# BELONGING:

## ISSUES OF EMOTIONAL LIVING
## IN AN AGE OF STRESS
## FOR CLERGY AND RELIGIOUS

# BELONGING:
## ISSUES OF EMOTIONAL LIVING
## IN AN AGE OF STRESS
## FOR CLERGY AND RELIGIOUS

## THE FOURTH
## PSYCHOTHEOLOGICAL SYMPOSIUM

BERNARD J. BUSH

KATHLEEN E. KELLEY

AUDREY E. CAMPBELL-WRAY

E. J. FRANASIAK

ANNA POLCINO

VIRGINIA O'REILLY

Edited by E. J. Franasiak

With a Foreword by Thomas A. Kane

## AFFIRMATION BOOKS
### WHITINSVILLE, MASSACHUSETTS

PUBLISHED WITH ECCLESIASTICAL PERMISSION

First Edition
© 1979 by House of Affirmation, Inc.

**Library of Congress Cataloging in Publication Data**
Psychotheological Symposium, 4th, Aquinas Junior College, etc., 1978.
  Belonging, issues of emotional living in an age of stress for clergy and religious.
      1. Catholic Church—Clergy—Psychology—Congresses. 2. Monastic and religious life—Psychology—Congresses. 3. Stress (Psychology)—Congresses. I. Bush, Bernard J. II. Franasiak, E. J., 1946- III. Title.
BX1912.P79 1978      248′.89      79-11482
ISBN 0-89571-007-2

Printed by Mercantile Printing Company, Worcester, MA
United States of America

To

present and former residents
of the House of Affirmation
with love and gratitude

# CONTENTS

# FOREWORD

To belong to another, to a family, to a group, and to God is among the deepest desires of all human persons. The person growing in affirmation knows and feels the strength and peace that belonging produces. Yet the risk of acknowledging our need to belong, in its beginning and in its end, depends upon trust in God. As Theodore Runyon reminds us in his compelling book, *What the Spirit Is Saying to the Churches*: "To trust God is to be enabled to trust oneself at the very core of one's being. . . . Once we have been grasped by God's affirmation of us, we have experienced love at the very heart of things, a love that cannot and will not let us go. And the power of that love begins to make all things in this fragmented world whole again."

The following poem was sent to me by one of the persons who attended the symposium on belonging. I believe her verses are well worth sharing.

## BELONGING

To belong with the free
Oh, pity me
For being so obstinate,
For not wanting to give in
To every politic and every whim
Of falsity and sin.

Oh, look at me
And see a rubble
Of sincerity and truth
Of trying to be brave
But only finding the aloof—

Oh, take me far
Away in a car, or on a star
Where I can dream
Again of things I've already seen
Of miracles anew
And real plans too
That more often than not come true—
For me and for you.

"God alone"—
He's so alone
If we never phone
To see if he's home—
In others . . .

Yea, we hunger
To be the other
Who is warmed by another
In hand, mind, or voice—oh, brother!
To see the shell
Of the infinite well
That goes deep I tell
In another . . . well . . .

"It's not right,
That you're out tonight."
Stay home and fight?
Or, "Turn out the lights."
It's only 8 o'clock.
It's time to set free
That Spirit in me
Which is the lover in me,
But where is every—body?
Gone to bed,
So hang your head
And just play dead
In your prison shed—

Unless—

You go
Slow—down
And catch the crown
That's above your frown
That beams and gleams
And gives forth streams
Of light, oh precious light
That puts to flight
All pretentious fright
And turns the night into
Broad daylight—hey lookout!
Here comes the Sun!

Sr. Carolyn Wilson, O.S.F.

Our ministry at the House of Affirmation is all about belonging. As a therapeutic community, our success depends upon our faith in Jesus and his power to heal and upon our ministry to one another. It is our hope, in this present series of essays, to share with other concerned persons some of our insights derived from our own religious experience, personal reflection, and clinical expertise. These essays are not meant to be definitive statements, but invitations for further reflection and sharing of scientific concerns.

The editor of these essays, Ed Franasiak, is one of the first lay persons who joined Sister Anna Polcino and me when we founded the House of Affirmation in 1970. We are indebted to him for his continual asking of challenging questions and for his deep sense of integrity, which he shares with his fellow staff members and with his clients. When we asked him to share in the founding of the House of Affirmation in California, he did so at great personal sacrifice and dedication marked by faith. It is with fraternal affection that I state that all who know Ed come to know something of the gentleness of Christ.

Affirmation Books, an important part of the ministry of the House of Affirmation, has grown rapidly over the last few years all around the world. One of our books has even been translated into Chinese! I hope that this new book entitled *Belonging: Issues of Emotional Living in an Age of Stress for Clergy and Religious* will meet with the wide approval our other publications have received.

It is with pride that I recommend these essays by my colleagues for your careful consideration and prayerful reflection.

Thomas A. Kane, Ph.D., D.P.S.
Priest, Diocese of Worcester
International Executive Director
House of Affirmation

January 19, 1979

# PREFACE

Again we have compiled the proceedings of the annual psychotheological symposium sponsored by the House of Affirmation, International Therapeutic Center for Clergy and Religious. And again because of gratifying audience attendance and response the symposium was held at Aquinas Junior College in Newton, Massachusetts, on October 7, 1978, and at the University of San Francisco, San Francisco, California, on November 4, 1978. This year's symposium was also held at Notre Dame High School in St. Louis, Missouri, on October 28, 1978, through the urging, support, and encouragement of the Sisters of St. Mary.

The topic for the annual symposium is chosen from among many topics suggested by participants of previous years' symposiums. Belonging furthers the previous themes of coping, loneliness, and intimacy. Thus this volume continues to raise questions about coping, the meaning of loneliness, and the possibilities of intimacy.

The essays in this volume focus on: the dynamics of restlessness and rootedness as dialectical forces in the process of belonging and creativity; the search for one's personal place in effective ministry and the risk of personal authority; belonging to a non-affirming, punitive God; the influence of sexual identity on our sense of belonging to ourselves, to one another, and to God, and the denial of homosexuality as a component of the spectrum of sexual identities; the goals, the ideals, and the pains of our attempts to belong with others in the deepest sense of oneness; and the necessary refinement of belonging in the middle years.

These topics represent some of the major questions of the modern world; so it is no wonder that religious, too, as they move more directly into the "ministry of the marketplace," are also being challenged to answer these questions —in ways that redefine and ascribe new meaning to their own religious lives.

In times of rapid change and stress, it is natural to search out our roots, our heritage, or the legacy we hope to pass to the future—our own and that of those whom we serve. We ask not only where we "belong" in a sense of connectedness and relatedness but where we "stand" on crucial human issues. These questions clarify where we are and with whom we achieve that undefinable but clearly sought sense that we are not alone, that we have a place from which to reach out and grow.

What becomes clear is that belonging is never achieved as a once-and-for-all. It is not an accomplishment, but rather a continuing refinement of our place in our environment, in our society, with others, and with God. When we stand as affirmed beings before God, the fullness of the life of grace can make us feel our place, our connectedness, our goodness, and our belonging.

I am grateful to Rev. James P. Madden, C.S.C., for moderating the Boston symposium, to Rev. Thomas A. Kane for moderating the St. Louis and San Francisco sessions, and to both of them for doing much of the laborious groundwork in preparation for these days. For the fourth year, the Sisters of St. Joseph made available their time and facilities at Aquinas Junior College in Boston. The St. Louis symposium would not have been possible without the time, effort, and interest of the Sisters of St. Mary. To both groups of religious women, I am deeply grateful.

Above all, I wish to thank the priests, sisters, and brothers who have come to the various centers of the House of Affirmation from various parts of the world to redefine their sense of identity, and who leave with the refined gift of themselves.

E. J. Franasiak
House of Affirmation
Montara, California

January 10, 1979

Rev. Bernard J. Bush, S.J., M.A., S.T.M., is director of the House of Affirmation in Montara, California. A member of the California Province of the Society of Jesus who was ordained in 1965, Father Bush studied theology at Regis College, Willowdale, Ontario. He served as student chaplain at the University of San Francisco before assuming the post of spiritual director at the Jesuit theologate in Berkeley, California. From there he went to Boston State Hospital where he interned in pastoral psychology. In 1974 he joined the staff of the House of Affirmation and opened its Boston office. Father Bush has written numerous articles concerning spirituality and social justice, most notably in *The Way*. He has been active in the directed retreat movement and has lectured on Ignatian spirituality, religious life, mental health, and social justice.

# BELONGING AND CREATIVITY

Bernard J. Bush

The notion of belonging is paradoxical. It contains the poles of a dynamic tension that we all feel and frequently are unable to articulate. One pole is the basic human need to be grounded, rooted, secure. Defining this need more precisely, we can speak of wanting to be self-possessed, grounded in reality, situated, integrated, confident, and at peace with our surroundings. The human sciences, particularly psychology, are the allies of this striving within us. These disciplines help us to identify and understand our needs and devise appropriate ways of satisfying them.

The other pole concerns the ideals of our Christian faith. Our faith tells us that the example of Christ should be the goal of our striving. Thus we are exhorted to self-forgetfulness, self-sacrificing service toward others, and meekness. We are told that we should turn the other cheek, forgive seventy times seven, return love for hatred, and ease our unrest through acknowledgement of our sins, true repentance, and forgiveness. Christ stated this paradox when he said, "The man who loves his life loses it, while the man who hates his life in this world preserves it to life eternal" (John 12:25).

Healing professionals feel this tension keenly because they know that ultimately death will take away all human health and sense of well-being. The paradox contained in the notion of belonging is not simply an intellectual abstraction. It is the very basic fact of life.

## BELONGING LEADS TO CREATIVITY

Hence the title of this chapter is "Belonging and Creativity." I see these two notions not as irreconcilable opposites, but rather as the tension polarities of the continuum of life. They are the stages, often repeated, in the flux of our journey toward our final destiny. In other words, there are times when we need the security of grounding, of settling, of feeling a wholeness within ourselves and solid relationships with external reality. There are also times when we need to face the void and chaos of the "not yet existing" and with great courage let go of the familiar in order to enter into the creative act of bringing in a new order, a new arrangement of things. Thus belonging is the indispensable precondition to launching creatively forth into the unknown. Teilhard de Chardin referred to this precondition in *The Divine Milieu* (London: William Collins, 1962):

> How would man give himself to God if he didn't exist?
> . . . develop yourself and take possession of the world
> *in order to be.* Once this has been accomplished, then is
> the time to think about renunciation; then is the time to

accept diminishment for the sake of *being in another*.
First develop yourself. . . .                    [Pp. 95-96]

This passage elucidates the theme of belonging and creativity. Our lives oscillate between meeting the needs and demands of the ego, the self, which are to be, to live, and to have a secure existence, and the demands of our life in Christ. He is, of course, the supreme example of what it means to live humanly. Taking the example of Jesus, we can say that his hidden and public life were the stages of belonging. He established his identity, gathered his disciples, located himself in temporal and sacred time and space. His death was the stage of diminishment, of letting go, of renunciation and self-sacrifice. It is important to note well the words of Jesus at this stage. He said: "I lay down my life to take it up again. No one takes it from me; I lay it down freely. I have power to lay it down, and I have power to take it up again" (John 10:17-18). Jesus understood the rhythm of belonging and creativity; he knew that he was not a mere victim of blind forces, but rather was free to enter into the process. The stage of creativity was his resurrection. In that mystery, he established a new and immeasurably higher life that includes all of us in his Mystical Body. In and through his experience, we all have the assurance that our experience will be parallel to his and will be as fruitful.

## SPATIAL BELONGING

Let us consider in more detail what is included in the experience of belonging. I think the experience suggests many things to each of us. Pause for a moment and think what comes to mind when you think of yourself as having a sense of belonging. One of the first ideas that generally suggests itself is spatial belonging—a place of one's own. In this personal space, one feels welcome, secure, and in familiar surroundings.

Possibly the most important space for me is my room. Think for a moment how personal this place is. What does my room contain? What mementos are there that remind me of my family and friends? What there reminds me of God, of the need to pray? A room is a highly personalized area reflective of who I am. Whether it is neatly ordered or in disarray, it is the place wherein I feel comfortable. Think about how uneasy we feel when we enter our rooms and by very subtle signs discover that some uninvited person has been there. We use our rooms as areas for retreat from pressure. Our rooms are the staging areas wherein we plan, think, and prepare ourselves to go out again to face the world of people and tasks.

Generally, when we do go forth from our rooms we bring things with us that connect us to our places. Think of what is in our pockets or purses. What items of personal significance do we carry that give us a sense of security? Certainly, having the keys to our houses or rooms is important. These keys are a connector to our space that allows us in and keeps others out. We are all familiar with the anxiety Linus experiences when he is deprived of his blanket. We all have something of this anxiety in us. In fact, we generally call our possessions our "belongings." When we lose them or have them taken from us, we feel as if we have lost something of our very selves.

Another space in which one has a sense of belonging is one's body. It is vitally important that we each have a sense of comfortable security in our bodies. Our bodies are places we always have with us. Body space is unique in the deepest sense. I and I alone dwell in that space. Obviously, if there is not a harmonious peace and reconciliation between a person and his or her body, that person will be constantly uneasy. In the same way, we need to appreciate and even reverence our bodily functions in order to be at peace within ourselves. This appreciation must include sexuality. It is important for us to be sexually well informed and to accept our sexual rhythms and feelings as dimensions of our being that belong to us.

The same can be said for our faces. Have I accepted that my face belongs to me, or do I wish I looked differently? Our faces are the windows to our souls. Through them our inner radiance shines through and delights others.

The paradox of spatial belonging is particularly intense. Place, possessions, and bodily space are vitally important to our sense of personal security and peace. Unfortunately, our society and culture, based as it is on consumption, preys upon our insecurity in this regard. We are told that only by amassing more and better belongings and by cultivating bodily beauty and pleasure can we be truly happy. There is an element of truth in these claims, but we must not accept them uncritically. The Christian ideals of dispossession, poverty, and bodily discipline also should be cultivated, but they, too, can be destructive in excess. Some ascetical practices lead us to believe that materiality is *per se* evil, particularly in relation to the body. An athletic asceticism designed to subjugate the body through ruthless discipline can result in a kind of civil war between body and soul. Obviously, what we need is a balance. We must cultivate harmonious cooperation before we can consider spiritual self-transcendence.

## TEMPORAL BELONGING

Another important ingredient in the sense of belonging is having a place in time. We are all located in history. There is a popular resurgence these days of tracing roots and genealogies. People seem to want to know where they have come from and who their ancestors were. Somehow the achievements or failures of our forebears tell us something of what we can expect from ourselves. This sense of historical belonging exists on many levels, and all are important. There is a continuity between the past and the present. Each generation has a heritage that it is expected to carry on and improve upon. Thus we are part of a family history, a national and state history, and a community, diocesan, and church history. Each of us is simultaneously carrying on temporal and salvation history. Our position in each of these histories has its own meaning and expectations for us personally. Each level of history we are part of bears down upon us with duties and responsibilities. All of this history gives us a specific place in time and shapes our sense of belonging.

Even our participation in this symposium bears on our sense of belonging. For example, each of us knows that he or she belongs in this auditorium for the day. We each made a reservation that entitled us to belong here. We were recognized at the door by the tickets we held. Thus we secured our personal spaces here. It is evident how important that space is to each of us personally. The vast majority of participants have staked a claim to a certain seat. Even though we have had a break and a period for lunch, most have returned to the same seats, for those seats have become for each participant his or her place, in which he or she belongs. Some may even have left something personal on their seats so that everyone else would recognize and honor those seats as belonging to them.

Thus recognition by others gives a sense of belonging. We all know how good it feels when someone remembers our names. We also know that moment of anxiety and near panic when we enter a room full of strangers. Is it not interesting that very often when strangers meet, they begin asking, "Do you know so and so from your community or diocese?" We try to find connections with others to establish how they somehow belong in relation to ourselves.

Other elements of belonging include our positions in our religious communities, dioceses, clubs, schools, parishes, etc. Besides these positions, we each possess unique talents and abilities that belong to us and help to make us secure. All people feel a sense of disorientation and drifting if they do not believe they are good for something. It is evident that we are involved in a veritable web of connections to people, places, times, and things that locate us and from which we derive our sense that we belong and of where we belong.

## BELONGING AND CHANGE

It is our profound experience and sometimes deep anguish that belonging is not the same as permanence. Once again a paradox enters the discussion. Quite simply, the sense of security, peace, and well-being that is gained from a firm sense of belonging is always being threatened. In fact, it is always in the process of being destroyed by change. The Greek philosopher who said we never put our feet into the same river twice was right. There is a tension in this fact of life. It is the purpose of this chapter to suggest that creative action springs from the tension between what we are and what we are becoming, between what we have and what we are losing or receiving. It is the tension between life and death and new life.

Artists, poets, and saints understand this tension best. Augustine said simply, "Our hearts are restless until they rest in thee." Shakespeare creatively reflects on the anguish of this condition in his Sonnet 64. I quote the last four lines:

> Ruin hath taught me thus to ruminate
> That time will come and take my love away.
>   This thought is as a death, which cannot choose
>   But weep to have that which it fears to lose.

The poet asks: since time will inevitably take my love away, what is the use of loving? Where is there any belonging if ruin makes everything impermanent? We will inevitably lose that which we seek to possess. St. Paul expresses this thought graphically in his first letter to the Thessalonians: "You know very well that the day of the Lord is coming like a thief in the night. Just when people are saying, 'Peace and security,' ruin will fall on them with the suddenness of pains overtaking a woman in labor, and there will be no escape" (5:2-3).

If we are truly in tune with the process, we will find that there is a kind of permanence even in the change. The process is one of transformation of a value to another value rather than one of an annihilation of one value with replacement by another. The simple truth is that we can move with peace to other places if we have ever found a place for ourselves. The pilgrimage motif for life means that we can find a home anywhere if we have felt at home somewhere. With strong roots, we can be transplanted and have real communion with all other places.

## PREMATURE RENUNCIATION

From what I have said, I hope it is clear that a sense of belonging and self-possession is required before renunciation can lead to new creation. Premature renunciation is deprivation rather than self-sacrifice. One problem many religious professionals face is that they never possessed what they have given up. Many entered the "state of perfection," as religious life is sometimes called, before passing through the normal developmental stages of imperfection. Scriptual evidence tends to support the fact that God does not demand renunciation from those who have nothing to start with. God always seems to call people out from a place. Witness Abraham who was called forth from his father's house and lands. The experience of Moses and the prophets was the same. The life and parables of Jesus reveal a similar pattern. Jesus himself lived an ordinary life for thirty years before he began the mission that he described as "having no place to lay his head." He called his disciples from their places, the fishing boats, the tax collector's booth, the fig tree, the wealth that was so hard to surrender, and so on. The parables illustrate what he lived. We know the stories of the grain hoarder who attempted to settle permanently in his comfort, the talents that had to be risked to gain more, and the rich man who feasted and refused to share with the beggar Lazarus.

The lesson seems clear. Voluntary renunciation and self-sacrifice require that there be something or some place to give up for the sake of something else. This process is the essence of all growth. In fact, if we are unable to sacrifice, we will become prisoners of places, possessions, or developmental stages. Ultimately, we will still lose what we had, but we will lose it uncreatively.

## CREATIVITY

Creativity is born out of the tension between stability and change. It is the result of entering into and freely cooperating with the process of shaping what is coming to be. A person is creative not by simply sitting back as a spectator to what is happening, but by being actively engaged in bringing forth the new and original.

Resistance is a common reaction to the emergence of the creative. Let us consider for a moment the great discoveries of astronomy and exploration. The world view of the late Renaissance, supported by philosophy and theology, was that the earth was flat and the sun and planets were in orbit around the earth. There was resistance to the ideas and even persecution of those who advanced a different theory. After all, how could Christ be considered the Lord of the Universe if he had not become incarnate at its center? Does not Sacred Scripture reveal that the sun goes around the earth? These dubious theological propositions were the source of much personal and historical anguish. Eventually, men realized that Scripture is not intended to be a source of scientific truth concerning planetary motion.

Similarly, in our own time the explorations of outer space have raised the possibility of extra-terrestrial intelligent life forms. If such life is encountered, our theological concepts concerning redemption, for example, will have to be modified. Inner space consciousness is also expanding. Genetic research is posing many questions that challenge our accepted notions of what life itself is and have caused us to seriously reconsider our moral and religious values. In ethics, as well as in every other area of human experience, great changes are taking place. This creative ferment is proceeding at an ever-accelerating pace. The rapid yielding of the old and the familiar to the new is a source of much stress and anxiety to all of us.

When we reflect on these changes and attempt to make the necessary adjustments to accommodate them, we must continually search out what is constant and enduring. Our idea of what is essential and permanent and what is accidental and transitory is always undergoing revision. In order to be truly creative, we must search out the essential meaning of things, as a painter tries, for example, to express the essence of a tree. Seen in this light, creative activity is a yearning for the eternal and the immortal. We try to express what is enduring, even clothed in a new, transitory form.

The creation of new forms requires passionate involvement and engagement. Apathetic creativity simply does not exist. Creativity requires a profound caring about what is happening. We must mind what is going on since we ourselves are in and of the process. In other words, we are committed to the pursuit of truth with a feeling of purpose. We as religious professionals are above all dedicated to this search. However, the moment of creative inspiration frequently occurs during a period of rest or relaxation. Oftentimes the solution to a problem occurs during a dream or when our minds are turned to other things. Thus periods of intense concentration, study, work, pondering, and involvement, alternating with periods of leisure, solitude, diversion, and play, are vitally necessary for a creative life. Each person must discover for himself or herself what rhythms are necessary in order to be personally creative.

Creative inspiration often is experienced as an irruption of the irrational. New forms clash with the ones they are replacing. Belief that the world was flat was a comfortable, accepted fact. The notion that the world was round seemed irrational. Yet the latter idea gave a new sense of wholeness and rightness. Data that was ignored previously or put out of consciousness because it would not fit finally had a place to be.

The inner creative experience can be personally very distressing. Perhaps anxiety describes the moment prior to the act of creation. The emerging is felt as an emergency. We seek relief from the distress. We are tempted to grasp more firmly what we feel slipping away. Anxiety itself has many forms, and it is generally an unpleasant sensation. However, I always consider anxiety a signal or warning feeling. It is the herald of something struggling to be born. Sometimes it is related to the past, as, for example, a painful memory that needs to surface and be reworked. Sometimes anxiety points to the future, as a new and unfamiliar challenge that threatens us when we confront it. In either case, we should listen to the anxiety and try to grasp what it is saying to us. Anxiety is a "not yet" experience, the moment of indecisiveness between letting go the old and grasping the new, between dying and rising. I fear that much creativity is lost to us because we so quickly run away from or anesthetize our anxieties.

A truly creative act is an original production of some kind. Something unique and personal comes into being. That something can be a thought, a solution to a problem, or a new synthesis of previously existing material. It must, however, be felt as something original to self. The implications of the new may not always be clear, but a feeling of satisfaction and joy in the new harmony is produced. In the life of the Church, the second Vatican Council stands out as a great example of creativity as I have just described it. Obviously, creative activity need not always be so dramatic. Discovering a new way of seasoning food can be a quite creative experience. And yet we often feel that the creative act is somehow beyond our powers or abilities. It is a moment of higher synthesis, an experience of self-transcending behavior. Mystical experience as the highest form of creativity is clearly understood to be God's work in and through the person receiving it. All other creativity has something of the same quality.

## VERTICAL CREATIVITY

The model I have been using for the movement from belonging to creativity might be seen solely as a description of the horizontal dimension of life. I have been speaking largely of the actualizing of our own personal human potential and of the way it leads to our expansive creativity into the world around us. This movement occurs within the limitations of history, space, and matter. Creativity also simultaneously takes place on what could be called the vertical plane. Creativity of this kind is not bound by the limitations of matter since it is spiritual and eternal. I am referring to the destiny of everything that exists to be transformed somehow into the divine. St. Paul lived with this vision and had a very hard time describing it. We need only recall the many eschatological texts of his letters. For example, in his letter to the Romans he says: ". . . the world itself will be freed from its slavery to corruption and share in the glorious freedom of the children of God. Yes, we know that all creation groans and is in agony even until now" (8:21-22). The Book of Revelations throughout sounds the same theme: "Then I saw new heavens and a new earth. The former heavens and the former earth had passed away . . ." (21:1). Much of the problem of grasping vertical creativity stems from its occurring in a way that is hidden from our usual ways of understanding or learning. St. Paul proclaims: ". . . if anyone is in Christ, he is a new creation. The old order has passed away; now all is new! (2 Cor. 5:17). In his letter to the Colossians, he sounds the same theme: "After all, you have died! Your life is hidden now with Christ in God" (3:31). Mystics and religious visionaries have found themselves occasionally transported into this spiritual realm by an extraordinary intervention of God. The effects of such experiences in their lives are very profound. The ultra-normal and supernatural become the norm of reality for them. In his "Contemplation for Attaining Love," St. Ignatius of Loyola suggests a way of praying that will open a person to receive spiritual awareness of the immanent presence of divine reality. In that exercise he proposes that I gratefully contemplate God working and laboring for me personally in all of created being (*Spiritual Exercises*, 230-37). As a lover to the beloved, God has given me all I am and have; so I ought to offer and return all to him. St. Ignatius of Loyola described the end result of contemplation in his own life as simply "whenever he wished, at whatever hour, he could find God" (*Autobiography*, 99).

There is a danger that, through concentration of effort and research toward understanding and producing the normal, well adjusted, and healthy, our human sciences will "psychologize away" the impulse to spiritual creativity and self-transcendence. On the other hand, there is abundant evidence that attempts to build a spirituality not firmly rooted on a sound personality structure can be even more dangerous. The movements from belonging to creativity on both the horizontal and vertical planes must take place simultaneously. The entire process of human development then becomes the stage of belonging that must be left for creativity in relationship to the spiritual and divine. These simultaneous movements are not in contradiction to one another. Rather, they can be visualized somewhat after the manner of planetary motion. The earth revolves on its own axis producing particular rhythms and cycles of night and day and all the seasons. These alternations produce the climate for life and growth. At the same time, the moon orbits the earth and together we orbit the sun. On a much vaster and incomprehensible scale, the entire solar system is somehow orbiting the galaxy.

When we use a model that takes into account movements within movements, it is easier to see how life moves on various levels and planes. I believe that under ordinary circumstances the call to a deepening awareness of the reality of God in our lives can be responded to consistently and with progress when the human is developing properly according to its own laws. In other words, the foundation of solid spiritual growth is good mental and emotional development.

We can feel the urge to transcend the self in spiritual growth as a kind of anxiety. Francis Thompson's poem, *Hound of Heaven*, is a classic description of this feeling. Thompson describes how he was pursued by a feeling that his ordinary life's preoccupations and activities were chains and avenues of escapes preventing him from developing the spiritual. Scripture is full of instances and descriptions of spiritual anxiety at the prospect of "leaving all" to grow in conscious relationship with God. Just as the gnawing feeling that accompanies physical hunger can be distinguished from similar feelings on a different level, such as "butterflies" or "stage fright," so spiritual anxiety is similar to other anxieties but has a different tone or quality.

St. John of the Cross has vividly described the particular fears, anxieties, and even terrors of the "Dark Night of the Soul." A person must be well grounded in the streams of life before he or she can risk entering the realm of spiritual creativity. The feelings I speak of here are substantially and qualitatively different from neurotic restlessness, free-floating anxiety, or obsessive, scrupulous perfectionism. Faith is the way of knowing truth on the vertical dimension just as reason is the way of knowing truth on the horizontal. The truth of faith is grasped through contemplation and discernment of spirits, while horizontal truth is grasped through reasoning and scientific investigation. We need to use all the ways of knowing in our lives in order to be creative in all the dimensions of life.

## CONCLUSION

We are all aware how important affirming gestures are to our sense of well-being. We all need to be shown in personally convincing ways that we are good and loved. In short, we need reassurances that we belong. Yet we know that these do not last. We receive them, are grateful for them, and draw strength from them so as to be able to reach out and share love with others as creatively as we possibly can.

Sister Kathleen E. Kelley, S.N.D., M.Ed., is career counseling director at the House of Affirmation in Whitinsville, Massachusetts. A member of the Boston Province of the Sisters of Notre Dame de Namur, Sister Kelley received her undergraduate education at Emmanuel College in Boston and did graduate work at Boston College. Prior to joining the staff of the House of Affirmation, she served on the province administration team and held the position of personnel director.

# WHERE DO I BELONG?

Kathleen E. Kelley

I chose a question as the title of this chapter for several reasons. First, the asking of questions is a way to approach life in an effort to discover its meaning. A questioning mind is an active mind: one that demands to know why things are as they are. When children engage us in endless question and answer sessions, we often conclude in exasperation that a thing is so simply because it is so. Perhaps children stop asking questions because we are unable to answer so many of them. Or perhaps we communicate by the way we answer certain questions that some topics are unsuitable for discussion. Eventually children get the message: stop asking and seek the answer on your own. If we could relive the experience of the child, both by asking the questions and by seeking the answers within us, we would move closer to the truth.

The second reason for posing my subject in the form of

a question is that all of the basic questions about life and about self never have definitive answers. Because we are in the process of growth, dealing with change within us and around us, the answers we arrive at at one point in our lives no longer fit the questions of a later period.

The specific question that I posed as the subject of this chapter had many variations in its formulation. When I attempted to explore the idea of belonging in the lives of religious and clergy, other questions surfaced: Why do I belong? How do I belong? Do I belong?

## THE HUMAN NEED TO BELONG

The need for a sense of belonging is not a question, for belonging is one of our primary needs as human beings. Needs are drives within us that demand satisfaction. We are all familiar with our basic needs for food and drink, and we are well aware of what happens to us when these needs are not met. We less readily acknowledge our needs for affection and belonging. Yet when these needs are not met, we suffer psychologically the same starvation and disease that affect us physically when we are deprived of food and drink. Once we satisfy our basic survival needs, we must then satisfy psychological needs such as belonging.

We all experienced this need as children. When we were in school, fitting in, being accepted by our peer groups, was important to us. We often changed our dress and/or behavior to achieve this sense of belonging. At home, we might have traded off what we really were in favor of what we thought we should be in order to achieve this same sense of belonging.

As we grow older, this need to belong remains with us because it is part of our human makeup. Failure to consciously recognize this need will not cause it to disappear. On the contrary, when unrecognized, this need assumes the form of an incessant and undefinable hunger within, a hunger that we mistakenly satisfy with food or drink or work. We must therefore learn to recognize this need to belong to self, to be rooted in a unique identity, to relate to someone in a meaningful way (intimacy), to join with others for some purpose (affiliation and achievement).

Many people, including religious and clergy, have difficulty thinking of themselves as needy people. We all prefer to be self-sufficient. We are uncomfortable with the idea of asking others to respond to our needs because it smacks of selfishness. So we make choices for supposedly altruistic reasons that may be far from our real reasons, and these choices often deny or ignore our human needs. We choose to help people because they need us, or we choose to stay in a job because the work needs us, when perhaps the real reason for our choice is our own need to be needed, to have a sense of belonging.

The question that entitles this chapter has been asked in one form or another by many of the priests and religious who have come to me with some very painful questions about themselves, their lives, and their work. Many come with questions about their ministry, expressing feelings of being overwhelmed, confused, and bored with life. Some come with vague feelings of uneasiness about themselves and their relationship—or lack of connection—to their work. All come hoping that if they change their work to something new or different their other problems will go away.

When I ask them to tell me specifically what type of working/living situation they are seeking, they very often draw a blank. Their reaction is not surprising. Many people do not know what they need as human beings to live happy, productive lives. They know only that something in their lives is not right and that, because life is not meant to be miserable, they therefore must seek a quick solution to their dissatisfaction. They look for a solution that answers for them the question : Where do I belong?

To answer this question one must first answer the questions: Who am I? and What am I meant to do with my life? Some persons experience feelings of unrest or vague uneasiness about themselves because their work—the "where" they belong—no longer satisfies or challenges them. But at the source of these feelings is the confusion that stems from not knowing who they are or what they are meant to do with their lives.

When we meet a person for the first time, we often ask where he or she is from, where he or she lives, or what place he or she calls home. In so asking, we identify "where" with a physical place. In this chapter, I do not intend to do the same. The physical place that we occupy or hail from is important, but it is not what I am addressing here. I am asking a question that was asked of the Lord, and I am looking at the way he answered it. When Jesus was asked where he lived, his response, "Come and see," named no street or town. His response implied that he lives where he is, that although he has no set physical place, he is at home anywhere.

I am asking where the space is in which each of us is at home: within ourselves, within our relationships, within our work. Is there a place where each of us in our unique identities can contribute our special gifts to life? I am asking where the place is where each of us can be known as who we are. If we know that place, if we have experienced belonging within ourselves and in what we do, we will possess that interior, private space, and we can bring it to any physical place.

When Yahweh demanded a special place for the Ark of the Covenant, he was asking the people to set aside a sacred spot where he would be known as who he was. Our own Christian heritage assures us that the Lord does not want us to demand individual arks! In fact, if we study the Israelites, we clearly see a people with no set place, a people wandering. Today we identify ourselves as a pilgrim people, willing and able to move from place to place, both responding to need and searching for God. But in order to sustain the demands of being a pilgrim people, helping others to find their unique places, we first must discover our own place. We must have a sense of belonging, an experience of rootedness, before we can branch out to serve others. If we do not discover our unique place—that space where we are at home—we can spend our lives in mission primarily searching for ourselves rather than serving others.

## ROOTS OF BELONGING

Certain elements of belonging and finding a right place are givens: we cannot choose them. Our family, our time in history, and our ethnic heritage are parts of ourselves that we cannot choose. We can choose only to derive a sense of belonging from them or to reject them. Until we choose to identify with these givens, however, they do not help us to find our unique place. Active, conscious choosing, then, is an element of discovering our place. Once we move from the realm of the givens of belonging to the realm of choosing to belong, we begin the search, and it is basically a search to discover our unique self and to accept that uniqueness as it flows into what we do.

We first discover that our unique place is not given to us gratis. We have to exercise the power within us to find that place wherein we are at home with our uniqueness, with our own richness. We then discover that the givens of belonging cannot forever be the sole fulfillers of our needs. Family and ethnic group can give us roots, but we must move beyond them if we are to grow and discover our adult place. Some persons who find refuge in these givens end up lost and rootless because the givens change. If we view priesthood or religious life as an extention of family or as a source of stability and security, we will have difficulty coping with the changes and the losses this life style causes in our personal lives. Although the givens in our lives do help to establish our basic identities, the choices we make to belong shape that identity.

Work constitutes a major choice in our lives because it can give us a sense of belonging and can be a strong formative factor in our identity growth. We very often experience a trial and error period when deciding where we fit in the work world. After graduation from school, we often move in and out of several different jobs looking for the "right one," for we look to work not only as a source of livelihood but also as a source of personal and relational growth. Many priests and religious, however, have bypassed this growth experimentation process and therefore have missed the identity clarification that results from it. Work is a means of self-discovery, and many theories have been advanced to define the relationship between who we are and what we do. Some theories hold that we become what we do. Others state that we choose what we do because of who we are. All theorists agree, however, that work and personal identity are dynamic forces that affect one another. It is this relationship that I believe is important in answering the question: Where do I belong?

## WORK AND BELONGING

Genesis records that "the Lord God took the man and put him in his garden of delight, to cultivate and tend it" (2:15). Thus man, as described in the full harmony of his being as a son of God, had a mission, a mission to work. Work, then, was a part of man's nature, one of the ingredients of his development of being. It was an act in which the whole person participated. There was no dichotomy between man's being and his doing. Man was, initially, in balance and harmony within himself and with the world around him. The mission to continue the work of creation was a gesture of bonding man to God. Disobedience broke the harmony, and thus the dichotomy between work and life began.

Part of the challenge of ministry today is to address that dichotomy: to learn to make choices that will foster harmony within us, ministry choices that flow from our needs, values, and interests. Frustration is a symptom of this dichotomy. Acute work frustration arises when there is no adequate outlet for the needs, values, and interests of the individual. If the work one does for forty hours—or, in so many cases, fifty or sixty or seventy hours a week—does not in some way give expression to who one is, then the dichotomy between being and doing persists.

It is difficult to deal with this issue because of the cultural emphasis on doing. We tend to define and stereotype people by the work they do. When asked what he or she does for a living, a person might at one time answer that he or she teaches second grade and at another time answer that he or she is a provincial. The change in what that person does affects both our opinion and definition of that individual, despite the fact the person is the same in either position. The person experiencing the change will in time respond to the role expectations of the two positions and will be thus shaped and modified by what he or she does. We must therefore decide what we want to become and how we want to belong to work, for otherwise we will be shaped by the choices of others in directions that may thwart our identity growth.

Since the relationship between work and identity is real, we must deal with part of that reality: our human needs. One of our basic work needs is to experience satisfaction and success. None of us can sustain consistent frustration and failure.

A growing number of studies being done on the relationship between work and human development suggest that persons need to feel a sense of effectiveness, termed psychological success. For an individual to experience this type of success, four conditions must be met: (1) the person must actively choose a challenging goal, one that will stretch the person to new levels of competence; (2) the person must work autonomously in trying to attain that goal so that the success will be the person's own and not someone else's; (3) the goal must be important to the individual's self concept; and (4) the person must achieve the goal.[1] If one measures these factors against the way many persons find their work in ministry, these persons' feelings of being misplaced and confused are more understandable. The measurement also poses a challenge for the future of ministry, for it reveals a connection between individual choice and ability to risk. If I choose my work, considering my talents and gifts in the context of authentic choice of ministry, and succeed, all well and good. If I fail, I have to deal with that reality. But if someone else chooses my goal for me and I succeed, I cannot claim that success as my own, and if I fail, I can blame the other for my failure and trade off my responsibility. Thus both success and failure involve risk and responsibility.

BELONGING FOR MINISTRY

For us as Christian people, the thrust of our work is clear: to continue the saving mission of Jesus. We clergy and religious persons have chosen to respond to the call to continue this mission. We live out this call through work that we name ministry. One of the primary reasons we choose to belong to the Church in a public way is for ministry, a ministry that should flow from our identities and contribute to them, a ministry that utilizes our unique talents and gifts. If ministry plays this part in our development, it should contribute then to our sense of belonging. If we have chosen work that integrates our doing and our being, we will know our right place. We will be able to spread the good news with joy. But such is not always the

---

1. Willis E. Bartlett, ed., *Evolving Religious Careers* (Washington, DC: Center for Applied Research in the Apostolate, 1970), p. 103.

case. Many of us have lost the joy because of the fatigue and pressure of work that is often ill chosen or done without any element of choice. Work is no longer lived as a means to an end, but has become an end in itself.

We make valiant efforts to read and respond to the needs of people as indicated by the signs of the times:

> Wherever God's name is not honored, wherever the daughters & sons of God are treated as less than persons, wherever institutions and societies oppress and exploit people and earth, wherever systems alienate people from themselves and from others, wherever sin and non-freedom are—there the church is called to be a visible and credible witness to the liberating love of God revealed in Jesus.[2]

Our work as priests, brothers, and sisters is for people. We seek to empower them to work toward liberating themselves from oppression. The needs of people can be overwhelming, and as we respond and involve ourselves, the needs seem to increase. The work is an endless task that will continue long after our part in it is finished. But because we are also part of a culture that likes to see things finished, a culture that works toward solutions and conquests, we find it difficult to sustain involvement in something that is endless, particularly if we did not choose our involvement. If we are not certain of our unique place in ministry, we can get lost in the scope of its demands. If we are not conscious of our own human needs, we run the risk of serving only ourselves in the name of ministry. If we are concerned with liberating the oppressed, of empowering others, we will be ineffective ministers if we have not

2. "The Role of Religious Orders in the Church's Ministry," *Origins* 7 (March 23, 1978): 637-38.

first looked at our own need to be liberated and our own use of power.

In our work, we may need to be liberated from a false idea of omnipotence. We may have to liberate ourselves from living the expectations of others or the assumptions of a community. The ideal priest and religious who can respond in all situations is simply not real. We may have to reexamine our gifts and talents and be freed from our expectation that we are capable of finishing the work. Whether my gift is that of being a superb teacher or of answering the telephone pleasantly does not matter. What matters is that I accept that gift and value it as my unique contribution, that I believe that gift is valuable simply because it is mine, and that I choose to work out of this reality.

Most of us are ordinary people doing ordinary work as part of an extraordinary mission. Of course, we all wish we could contribute something of extraordinary significance. It is something of a hard blow to us to accept the ordinary. But the ordinary is often where God speaks. Remember Elijah when he was looking for the Lord:

> A strong and heavy wind was rending the mountains and crushing rocks before the Lord, but the Lord was not in the wind. After the wind there was an earthquake, but the Lord was not in the earthquake. After the earthquake there was fire, but the Lord was not in the fire. After the fire there was a tiny whispering sound. When he heard this, Elijah hid his face. (1 Kings 19:9, 11-13)

Individuals who do not feel that they have found their place often fail to appreciate their own unique gifts. This failure is not hard to understand. Many clergy and religious entered seminary or novitiate at an age when identity was just beginning to become individualized. But the stress on group and conformity stopped the process. In time the persons were assigned their ministerial duties with critical elements missing: identity and choice. They were experiencing the developmental stage when identity should have been clarified through work, but that rarely happened because identity was not clear to begin with and work was not considered an area for identity clarification. Many results flowed from this situation. Some persons took on their full identification with and from their work, totally oblivious to their personal identities and to the human needs that formed part of those identities. To lessen the feelings of misplacement, they worked harder, dealing with the quality of their lives through the quantity of their work. Others endured their work, spiritualizing its personal effects and responding to its demands. They could not admit that they could not do their work, for they believed that God would help them. So they moved from one responsibility, masking insecurity, to another, accepting newer and greater responsibility to a point where no work was too hard. The variety of activities they were called upon to do enforced the feelings that there was little they could not do. Self-knowledge did not have a chance to exist. These people are now in the process of self-discovery and are searching for belonging.

The feelings these people are experiencing because of a lack of a sense of belonging, because of feelings of alienation, are touching them on various levels. Within themselves, they are restless and bored. They experience listlessness, sleeplessness/oversleeping, and/or increased/decreased appetite. They are disinterested in their work, and the effort to work does not make sense to them. They tend to blame anyone and everything in an attempt to identify the source of the problem outside of themselves. Some persons cope with these feelings by becoming work addicts. All must deal with acute loneliness, with the feelings that nobody cares. Some sit with these feelings waiting for someone to come and take them away. These persons want to find their place, to feel they belong, but without going through the work of searching. They prefer to be given their places gratis. They are overwhelmed with the reality that it is their personal responsibility and right to choose life. They consistently look to outside causes, bad assignments, or bad living situations, hoping for outside solutions. But outside solutions will not dispel the anxiety and distress that is within them as individuals.

For some persons, the outside solution rests with obedience to authority. But this level of obedience, to be authentic, must be preceded by the personal obedience of listening to who I am and accepting what gifts I have been given. The person has to deal with basic identity, with his or her needs, values, and goals, and realize that the power to so deal is within.

This history of the dichotomy of work versus identity existed for both men and women in the Church, but in different ways. Consequently, today men and women in the Church are dealing with different issues from similar origins. Work demanded of men a broad-based involvement in all facets of life. Men were expected to be confident and competent as pastors, administrators, preachers, and counselors, without any personal needs. They were given power to function thus through their roles. Now men in the Church are dealing with loss. When men who lack a sense of basic identity experience change in the work from which they gained identity, crisis and a sense of loss of place is inevitable. For women in the Church, work was clearly defined by very set parameters. The place of women was confined, and their power was restricted. Now women in the Church are dealing with gain. But they may also experience crisis. Women whose personal identity is vague and whose choice of work is totally open may get lost in the misuse of power.

## POWER AND AUTHORITY

Personal oppression and the realization and responsible acceptance of personal power are issues that must be dealt with when discovering identity in mission. Oppression is the misuse of power; so if we work at liberation, we must concomitantly work at using personal power responsibly. Power can be defined as energy. We were given power as human beings, when, in Genesis, man was mandated to name the beasts. To name is to have power over, in the image of God. In the act of creation, God empowered each creature with the freedom to use or not use that power. Power, then, along with the commission to work, is within human nature:

> Today, it is unreal in ministry to believe that we can enable another individual or group unless we are willing to take seriously the stewardship of our own power as a person. . . . Do not the injustices and oppression of the times demand ministry to be the enablement, the empowerment of individuals and communities to realize their own dignity and self worth, to perceive

their own options, to make their own decisions in self determination . . . ?[3]

Authority, on the other hand, is not a given. It has to be assumed. The use of power and authority over others can foster oppression if it does not flow from one's personal authority directing one's inner power. We are given, through creation and baptism, both freedom and responsibility. To responsibly accept one's power in freedom is essential for becoming a person. Each of us has the power within to author his or her own life responsibly. One of the tasks of ministry is to use power creatively, a power rooted in personal identity.

Until we not only deeply believe in but also act out of our personal power to author our lives, we will be poor teachers of others. This fact applies to both men and women. But within the Church, power has touched men and women differently. Men were given power of authority through their roles. Perhaps now they have to backtrack to root their power in personal authority, for we cannot justly use the power of authority over others if it does not flow from personal responsibility. Women must achieve the reverse. They have to believe that power is within them and then have the confidence to exercise it responsibly outside of themselves. Some women, in a move against oppression, have already gone outside of themselves with power and authority that is communicated through hostility and aggressiveness. If the power was responsibly rooted in their personal identities, there would be little need to prove that it existed.

3. S. Ethne Kennedy, ed., *Gospel Dimensions of Ministry* (Chicago: National Assembly of Women Religious, 1973), pp. 14-15.

After all, we are all struggling and searching to find our places in the ministry of the Church, and we are dealing with similar basic issues. The future suggests an expanding, changing concept of ministry that will be frightening for those who do not know who they are, who have not found that at-homeness within themselves from which they can move in any direction. Persons who do not first belong to themselves, in acceptance of themselves, are apt to wander from place to place in ministry looking for their homes. If we are rooted in the reality of who we are, facing the need for personal liberation and accepting our responsibility for personal power to author our lives, we can move closer to defining our place, to knowing where we belong.

A major part of the discovery of who we are is related to what we do. The knowledge and feeling that we are where we belong result from the arduous tasks of self-assessment and of actively choosing ministry. If we have found the place within ourselves where we accept the reality of who we are, then we can deal with the mobility and pressures of ministry without getting lost in them. If we know where our home is, where we can be known as we are, we will have grasped a sense of belonging that will flow into effective ministry. The personal aspect of the search for our unique place is important, for the search for our place of at-homeness is simultaneously a search for God who is our ultimate place of belonging.

When we speak of mission and ministry, we speak of witness—witnessing to the love of God for his people. In our parishes, schools, and hospitals, we have touched souls, minds, and bodies in response to needs. Are we not in a period of history in which there is a need for a witness to wholeness, in which the appreciation of all aspects of humanness are needed for integrating life? What then should our witness be today if it is not to wholeness of being, to the recognition that we are fragile, dependent, needy human beings who, because we believe in the presence of the Lord among us, risk life, and who, because we believe, can assure one another: wherever you are, you belong, because you take your own space with you?

Audrey E. Campbell-Wray, M.A., M.A.S., is ancillary therapies director at the House of Affirmation in Montara, California. In this capacity, she directs the art therapy, spirituality, and activities programs. Ms. Campbell-Wray brings to the staff of the House of Affirmation the richness of her Afro-American culture and a varied educational and experiential background. A native New Yorker, she attended Hunter College before completing a tour of duty with the U.S. Navy as a neuropsychiatric technician. She subsequently received an undergraduate degree in fine arts and psychology from Lone Mountain College, San Francisco; a master's degree in theology from St. John's University, New York; and a master's degree in applied spirituality from the University of San Francisco. In addition to several years of experience in psychiatric clinics, she spent two years as an art therapist with the Veterans Administration and four years as a Catholic high school religion instructor and retreat program coordinator. Ms. Campbell-Wray is currently doing doctoral studies in clinical psychology at the Psychological Studies Institute in Palo Alto, California. She is a member of the American Art Therapy Association, the American Society of Group Psychotherapy and Psychodrama, and the International Society of Artists.

# BELONGING TO A PUNITIVE GOD

## Audrey E. Campbell-Wray

When you belong, you have to see yourself as suitable, as a part of or in possession of someone or something. Belonging means you have a proper place and you are in a relationship. Belonging comes from the Old English *be*, meaning "completely," and the Middle English *langian*, meaning "go along with": completely go along with the God who says:

> I have loved you with an everlasting love.

and

> Behold I stand at the door and knock.
> If anyone hears my voice and opens the door,
> I will come in and sup with you and you with me.

This God says:

> *You are the suitable place for me.*
> I will possess your heart, and we will completely go along with one another forever.

But all too often your answer is NO, for that is not the voice of the god that you hear. Your god is a threatening and punitive god, and his voice threatens you thus:

You will obey the lord your god or else!

And you respond:

I will obey and appease this god;

I will serve and try to love him or else!

Instead of living as a child of God, you live as a child of fear, and you *create* your *punitive* god; and this punitive god grows only stronger

never wiser

never gentler

because you have fed and nurtured this god for years. Perhaps you will recognize the following as your song.

The part of me I do not like becomes my punitive god. My fear becomes my god. My pain becomes my god. My delusions and distortions become my god. My prejudices and lack of tolerance become my god. My belief that I am no good or not good enough becomes my god. My desire to beat myself, kick myself becomes my god. My need to be irresponsible toward my life, to make someone else responsible for what happens to me becomes my god. I know how to belong to this punitive god. *It is basically the way I belong to my punitive self.* This god is very close to me, and never lets up. Like an ever-present burden—with very large eyes. As soon as I see myself step out of line, I know that this god sees it too. If I feel miserable and hate myself, I know that this god hates me too. I am not acceptable, and I let him down; so why should he give anything to me?

THE GOD OF NO . . .

Then we hear the *sad psalm* of a *soul immersed in a punitive god:*

> You are a god of no-name, no-help, no-love, and no-care.
>
> I feel no protection, no parenting, no mutuality, and no understanding.
>
> You are a god of no-joy, no-life, and no-hope.
>
> You are a god who demands too much, and yours are not human demands, not even possible demands.
>
> You are a god of no-forgiveness, no-mercy, no-leniency, no-give-and-take.
>
> You are a god only of virgins, and of widows, and of martyrs.
>
> You are a god of no-peace, no-calm, no-reassurance, nor underlying certainty.
>
> So far away . . . where are you? I can't see you, touch you, or feel you.
>
> You are a god of no-light, and I cannot see in the darkness.
>
> I do not know which way to turn or in which direction to take a step.
>
> I am afraid of the dark, and you are dark.
>
> You are a god of no-light.

And so goes the psalm of a delicately unbalanced life, unaffirmed in his or her spiritual journey. It is not uncommon to find such a one besieged by various psychological and physical pathologies as well. It is therefore not surprising that many who come to the House of Affirmation for psychological assistance present also the punitive god syndrome. Theirs are lives without harmony.

Borrowing from Rollo May's comments on the neurotic process: such a one finds the *needs* but not the *resources*, finds the *questions*, but not the *meaning*. It is like the artist never able to complete the work of art, driven by conflict into perpetual irresolution, such that the whole experience leads to a loss of meaning and feeling. Meaninglessness. Feelinglessness. Despair. Apathy.

That depth of apathy in the wake of a loss of a possible personal love relationship with none other than god leads to religious magic and ultimately to a hidden atheism.

Religious Magic sounds like this:

> If I feel good, god is good.
>
> If I feel bad, god is bad.
>
> If I do not know whether I am good or bad, then either everything is good or everything is bad, and I just will not listen to god.
>
> Let god show me signs.
>
> I did nine somethings, and I still did not get *anything*.
>
> I had great devotions, enthusiasms, and sentimentalities, and *nothing* happened.
>
> I kept the rule, and the rule did not make me holy.
>
> I made vows; so I should not have to cope with these things.

Religious magic *ignores reality*. It looks for ways to bypass the process, the struggle, the tension, the sin, and the responsibilities of living our everyday lives.

Religious magic *ignores subtleties*. It looks for clear and extreme answers. It ignores humor, absurdities, nuances, and the unexpected.

Religious magic *seeks to control God*. It wants mastery

and seeks to ignore mystery. It seeks to limit God to the information you have and the solution you see.

Religious magic *leads to athesism*. It draws you away from relationship with a real and personal God who invites, and substitutes a relationship with fear and disillusionment. You end up with no one and nothing trustworthy in your belief system.

Religious magic and sentimentality can thoroughly *take the place of a serious journey to God.*

Religious magic causes us to *bypass discernment* so that very soon we cannot determine the difference between a genuine and a counterfeit experience of any kind.

The heart of the matter is that there is nothing in this punitive god syndrome to believe in. You have taken your punitive self-god and projected him up into the clouds and then asked him, like a puppet on a string, to dance a dance, to sing a song, and ease the pain. And the answer is resounding, empty S I L E N C E.

And *out of the silence steps weeping the Religious Orphan:*

I used to pray, but I cannot pray anymore.

I used to be very close to the Holy Mother, but she means nothing to me now.

I used to think of God as my Father, but now I am not even sure that he exists.

## THE RELIGIOUS ORPHAN

*The Early Psalm of the Religious Orphan*

This father is not my real father. God will be my father.

These children are not my real siblings. All people will be my siblings.

This home is not my real home. Heaven will be my home.

Nothing here is real. The real is yet to come. I will find it *after*, after this place, after this relationship, after this life.

There is something better. It is just beyond. I cannot grasp it. But I know it is there.

### The Middle Psalm of the Religious Orphan

I have come to a place of no-welcome. I have to be tested, sized-up, taught, restricted, and formed.

I did not belong out there. I am not sure I belong *here*. Maybe I belong nowhere.

I was born into a family, and I did not belong to it.

I was raised in a community, and I did not belong to it.

I entered a congregation, and I *should* belong to it.

I have been in many parishes and schools where I did not belong.

Even if I began to feel that I could belong, I would be moving along again in a year or so anyway.

Maybe all nuns, brothers, and priests are orphans searching for a home.

### The Later Psalm of the Religious Orphan

I have a God I do not belong to because I cannot suit him.

I cannot do anything right.

I have a Lord I cannot relate to. Jesus is my brother they say, but who can be like him—he was divine.

I cannot belong to the communion of saints
because I am a sinner.
I cannot build a kingdom of love because I hate
myself.
Where are my parents, my sisters, my brothers?
Where do I belong? Who loves me?
I am an orphan, and I am afraid. I am afraid to
tell you how I feel. I would be afraid to tell you
that I love you because I do not belong.
I have to protect myself from you, from life, from
God.
I am afraid that I will be punished. And I am
punished by my fear.

BELONGING

Could it be that the religious orphan belongs nowhere—
not heaven, not earth, not hell?

Could there be such a one who is possessed by no one, part
of nothing, who has no proper place, no suitability, no
relationship, and no membership?

Could it be that a religious orphan presented to Jesus will
hear: "My friend, your sins are forgiven," which is one
way of saying "Pick up your mat, and *completely go along
with me, forever.* And so that you might know that you
*belong with me forever* I tell you, and *it should make you
feel better*, your sins are forgiven." This is the invitation of
the real and personal Jesus who wishes to tell you that his
*love is more important than suffering.* My love offers

*resources* to your *needs.*

*meaning* to your *questions.*

*soothing* to your *fears.*

*healing* to your *wounds.*

This is the God speaking whom you DO NOT KNOW.

## TRANSFORMING THE PUNITIVE GOD

### *The Bridge*

If you reach only into the air, it is too lofty, too airy, ungraspable, ambiguous, no-name, no-substance, no-reality. And you splinter and float away, off in bits and pieces.

If you have not touched down upon the earth, how can you belong to it, or find yourself thousands of feet into it, where you can grab hold and *know who you are*, feel yourself, embrace your being, hear your language, connect with your ancestors, your siblings, and your very own soul, your very own *humanity?*

The Bridge is the earth and the gift of life past, present, and future. You do not have to navigate this bridge alone. It is only partly your work. Partly, it is God's—the One to whom you belong. YOU ARE THE SUITABLE PLACE FOR HIM.

While we empty ourselves of our punitive God, we may seem inattentive to the Good God—strangers—but he will heal and nourish as is his nature—though we are unconscious of it. Then we can gradually move into awareness of that healing, nourishing God because that process of becoming aware is also his work. Look at the bridge symbolically as a roadway to transformation. Reflecting on deeply rooted symbols, you can call *Thunder, Mystical Rhythms,* and *Universal Soul.* You can see a transformation that takes place in the earth, in the genes, and in the experiences of life. These mini-dramas can be looked at as reflectors of the major drama taking place between you and God—your transformation.

Consider the thunder; you must hear the booming, shattering sound of thunder, sometimes frightening, but also fascinating, loud, strong, and relentless. It shakes buildings and causes parents to hold and comfort their children; it sometimes strikes down trees, sometimes kills, and always is accompanied by waters to replenish the earth and the people. The Thunder far off sounds not like a roar, but like a beating drum that is seductive and inviting. It is a sound to follow; it attracts. It is the beating of the path to step toward something greater than yourself. The closer you approach, the more the beat becomes a roar and the louder the roar within you, the more like Thunder you become.

Consider the Mystical Rhythms; there is motion to contend with. There is movement both inside and outside space and time. It is the dimension in which union, healing, touching, and contemplation are to be found. The rhythms change; they are fast and slow; they reach highs and lows. It is in response to the Mystical Rhythms that a person facing death can be consoled by a vision of eternity, or that the ocean or a blade of grass can represent the expansive mysteries of God, or that a lover can step outside of self long enough to make passionate love to someone else, or that a monk can center the entire day and night around periods of prayer. The more attention you give to the Mystical Rhythms, the more like them you will become.

To consider the Universal Soul, it is essential to step out of solitude. The Universal Soul symbol is communal. It connects me to you, and us to all others. It accounts for concern about our ancestors as well as for our sisters and brothers across the face of the earth. It accounts for the desire to care for our fathers' graves, a hungry child's stomach, a war-torn nation, a mentally or physically helpless neighbor. Universal Soul causes us to chronicle our histories, even to the point of making ourselves sound better to the next generation than we really were. It causes us to account for the missing-in-action and the politically, racially, and religiously oppressed. It impels some to fast for other peoples' causes and jeopardize their futures for other peoples' rights. It makes us one family from ancient times to now, from East to West, North to South. The more you deeply reflect upon the implications of the Universal Soul symbol, the more like it you become.

The bridge is the gift of ongoing life. You transform the punitive god by the transformation of your punitive self. You celebrate that gift of life through your connection to the God of eternal life. Consider the idea of God's attributes as developed by St. John of the Cross in *The Living Flame of Love*. God actualizes God-likeness in people who respond or open themselves to receive his gift— himself. If you allow God's goodness to enter and enlighten you, that very action transforms you in part or whole into that goodness; then in some way, principle, or part you have become like God.

## *The Touch*

You move across the bridge to a place of harmony— earthly, physical, psychological, spiritual harmony. Where "thy will be done" is not a request but a longing for what God alone can do—a god who is not an idol, who is not merely one thing among many. God alone can touch the substance of the soul. And when other things awaken or remind you of that touch, there will be peace, joy, and love. When something disrupts it, there will be disharmony.

Learning to live with the power of God's love is no easy task. Believing and living as if God is capable of doing his work can be very difficult for those who secretly seek mastery and control. God's word is sufficient to accomplish his work, and his love is more powerful than our problems. It is often through the holes of our weaknesses and failures that the love of God can pour into our lives. Be willing to wait for confirmation in time and in space; look for the effects of love, new life.

The nature of love is such that it must be shared, spoken, and expressed. Unspoken love is dry and unfree and becomes the source of heartaches, or, worse yet, of secret weapons for destruction, because the other did not know your expectations or the delicate intensity of your feelings. There is a flow to a love relationship. And whether the other is your sister or your brother or God, it is the same transforming love that moves and grows and flows. It is sometimes helpful to analyze an experience in steps, not because it happens that way but because the steps help us understand the experience. So we can examine our journey in this manner:

The *fantasy level* is the imaginative and joyful stage when excitement is alive and adventure is at hand. The ideas flow and the dreams give sensible delight. But there is more.

The *playful level* is the lively stage when laughter buoys the spirit and energy is actually spent on joy. But there is more.

The *sharing level* is for knowing one another; it is not for entangling the other in a web of your own needs, but for a mutual interest in who the other actually is. Here our love relationships with friends and with God often break down or stagnate because we do not want to ground ourselves in the reality of truly knowing another person whether or not he or she can satisfy our felt needs. The time comes when we must choose God because of who God is in himself—pleasure or no pleasure. But there is more.

The *caring level* means giving, speaking out when necessary, doing when needed, helping, showing affection and compassion, being available, and healing with skill and love. But there is more.

The *movement level* compels growing and flowing toward maturity and real wholeness. It compels accepting useful change and wise guidance. But there is more.

Finally, there is *closeness and time* spent in peace, delight, and joy. But even then, there is more.

## THE PUNITIVE GOD TRANSFORMED

I have found you in your suitable place, dear God, my heart.

You alone can melt this heart with the fire of your love.

Mine is melted, and joyful and free.

I am one who belongs, has a proper place, and is in your possession.

I can choose to be whole and human;

I can decide to completely go along with you, forever.

I am firmly fitted to the earth with all that you have given me, with all that I have made of it, with all that I have blemished.

I am also lifted by your love.
You are a God of transformation and of life.

When I am afraid, I will try to hear what you have told me: "I was with you then; I am with you now; I will be with you later."

When I have betrayed you three or maybe twenty times, I know you will ask only, "My friend, do you love me?"

And for my part, I will make a place for you to have a gentle rest. I will make the space for closeness and for time. I will do my best.

And still there is more.

Ed Franasiak is a psychotherapist and assistant director of the House of Affirmation in Montara, California. He studied at St. Bonaventure University, Olean, New York; Assumption College, Worcester, Massachusetts; and the International Graduate School of Behavioral Science in Switzerland. He received his master's degree in psychology from Boston College in 1971. He is now a candidate for a doctoral degree in clinical psychology at the Psychological Studies Institute, Palo Alto, California. He is a member of the American Psychological Association and the California State Psychological Association.

# HOMOSEXUALITY AND RELATED MYTHS OF *UN*BELONGING

E. J. Franasiak

Several months ago I was talking to a friend of mine, a woman who is in a religious community and who at the time was posing some difficult questions about her religious vocation. I mentioned to this friend that belonging was the theme for this year's symposium and that my presentation dealt with homosexuality. My friend looked puzzled. "Ed," she said, "What does homosexuality have to do with belonging?" I tried to give her some explanation of my understanding of the relationship between homosexuality and belonging, but it was obvious that my friend was not listening. Finally, she interrupted me saying, "I'm having such a hard time dealing with my strong heterosexual feelings at this point in my life that I just can't believe that homosexuality is a problem or even a topic of any interest among religious."

Then again one priest told me, "It doesn't matter to me

if I'm heterosexual or homosexual because I'm a celibate anyway.'' What a sad statement! I do not need to know whether the pastor in my parish labels himself a ''heterosexual'' or a ''homosexual.'' I do not even believe that there are just these two kinds of people. However, in 1978 I need to know that my pastor is struggling or growing with his sexual identity like I am and like my friends are. I did not need this reassurance in 1958. Today I need to know that my pastor is a fully human person and that part of his humanity is a growing and vital sexual identity. I need to know that his celibacy is embraced as a life-giving gift, not as a substitute for human loving concern or human sexual energy.

As a psychotherapist who works primarily with religious men and women, I believe that in the last five or ten years these men and women have achieved a heightened and healthier personal sexual awareness. They have manifested a deeper integration of sexual feelings, a clearer perception that sexuality belongs to each and every human being.

## LIMITED SCOPE OF TOPIC

Because the topic of homosexuality is both complex and emotionally charged, I have found it necessary to set some limits on the scope of this chapter. First, I am not going to attempt to review the literature on the subject of homosexuality. Almost every reader is able to think of a recent piece of writing that enabled him or her to gain some kind of perspective on the subject. Second, I will not offer my opinion about specific problem areas of homosexuality, such as questions concerning homosexual feelings and living in same-sexed communities, how a community of religious can deal with an individual who identifies his or her homosexuality, or what a religious professional who experiences homosexual feelings does. Much helpful material addressing these questions has been written. Moreover, to take such a problem-directed approach to homosexuality would be to continue to see it in a reductionistic way, removed from the deeper realm of human experience. A reductionist approach stereotypes homosexuality as pathology and accomplishes little in understanding it.

This approach also reduces homosexuality to a narrowed focus of genitality and fails to consider it in terms of relationship. This approach confirms that homosexuals do not belong in loving relationships. One sister admitted to me: "As soon as I hear the word 'homosexual,' I immediately think of genital activity. But when I hear the word 'heterosexual' I think of relationships. I think there's something wrong with that."

Indeed, homosexuality is a loaded word whose implicit connotations are often negative and anxiety producing. Thus I do not propose to discuss the pathology of homosexuality. Rather, I wish to consider feelings and ideas about homosexuality. My intention is neither to condone nor to condemn the phenomenon of homosexuality. I intend, instead, to invite reflection on how most people think about homosexuality and how some people feel about it. By taking this reflective approach, I hope to refine some of our perceptions of homosexuality. After all, our understanding of the intricacies of psychosexual development, especially in regard to the phenomenon of homosexuality, has less influence on our reactions to an individual homosexual than do our attitudes and feelings about this emotion-laden issue. Our anxiety, fear, contempt, *or* acceptance and love will determine whether homosexuals "belong" in our society or our religious communities.

## LACK OF UNDERSTANDING CAUSES CONFUSION, ANGER, AND ANXIETY

I propose that homosexuality as it is generally defined is based on an inadequate understanding of what it means to be "masculine" and what it means to be "feminine." It is further based on an inadequate understanding of how these two aspects, the "masculine" and the "feminine," join in a single human personality. This inadequate understanding leads us to perceive the man or woman who does not measure up to stereotypic definitions of "masculine" or "feminine," or who does not measure up to the established patterns of development, as not belonging to the general population in the way he or she is *supposed* to belong. Because our understanding is inadequate, we perceive these persons as outside the norm. We thus perceive homosexuality in a limited way that too easily relegates it to the closet of pathological definition.

Of course, homosexuality is—to some degree—a problem. But the problem is not necessarily that of the labeled "homosexual" person. Homosexuality is a problem because it has become so controversial. It has been brought to our attention in the political arena and in the media. It has become a popular subject of scientific, theological, and psychological literature. Accompanying this growing interest in homosexuality are strong and divergent opinions, frequent theoretical confusions, and heated arguments. It even seems that a sizeable bibliography can be compiled to support and substantiate whatever viewpoint toward homosexuality that one chooses to hold. The end result for people in leadership positions, pastoral ministry, or the helping professions, and for any person struggling with a developing sexual identity, is a gut-level feeling of confusion and questioning of previously held beliefs.

Anxiety frequently accompanies these angry and confused reactions. People often get very uptight when homosexuality is the topic of conversation. It seems that homosexuality causes very deep-seated anxiety among many people in our culture. Marc Oraison, the noted French psychiatrist and theologian, writes that the issue of homosexuality challenges affectivity "mainly on an unconscious level."[1] When people are touched at this deep, unconscious level, they naturally exhibit some signs of anxiety. This experience of anxiety contributes most to perpetuating the "myth of *un*belonging."

For example, recently I was listening to a talk show on a San Francisco radio station during which a set of parents, a representative from the homosexual community, and the host were discussing a local political proposition to bar identified homosexuals from teaching in public schools. The woman was adamant about barring homosexuals from teaching her children. In asserting her strong position, she exhibited a classic Freudian slip. She meant to say that if the proposition were not passed, more children would inevitably lean toward homosexuality because of the influence of their homosexual teachers. But the woman said that the children would "inhale" homosexuality from their teachers, as if homosexuality were a contagious virus the children could contract by breathing. On a conscious level,

---

1. Marc Oraison, *The Homosexual Question* (New York: Harper and Row, 1971), p. 29.

this woman was deeply angry. But her unconscious fear and anxiety were even greater and deeper. She is perhaps typical of a large number of people in our society who are equally anxious about homosexuality. Today we are experiencing not so much an epidemic of homosexuality as an epidemic of anxiety concerning homosexuality.

## CATEGORICAL THINKING
## CONTRIBUTES TO THE PROBLEM

Why do some people experience such anxiety? One reason is that at the intellectual level the concept of homosexuality causes a kind of dissonance, a conflict with preconceived categories. It does not fit into prior conceptual schemes of "normal" or "natural." By default, then, it is relegated to a closet of pathological behavior.

Because categories are built into our language, they are implicit in the way we perceive and describe our reality. Because of the limitations of language, we are accustomed to thinking in categories—usually dichotomous—such as normal versus abnormal, natural versus unnatural, and heterosexual versus homosexual. When a perceived reality is categorized in this way, we find it very difficult to change our perceptions of that reality even when new knowledge surfaces. Recall, for example, the turmoil many people felt when blacks demanded integration and when women refused to remain subordinate to men. Because our emotions often lag behind our intellect, we allow our attitudes and prejudices to become entrenched, and we accept them as self-evident givens. Intellectual knowledge almost always precedes emotional acceptance of this knowledge, sometimes by years and even decades. Our anxiety about homosexuality is rooted in this emotional lag.

When it is applied to people, categorical thinking creates anxiety. Categories are more appropriate to objects of scientific research. When they are used to describe people, they alienate. When we categorize, we separate. With the category "homosexual," we set a whole group of persons apart. The person who categorizes himself or herself as "homosexual" also feels apart, as one who does not belong. The category perpetuates the anxiety and emotional alienation of the homosexual person in society in general and in religious life in particular.

When people are mutually defensive, they feel in opposition to and unaffiliated with one another. They have no sense of belonging to one another. "Homophobic" is a word used to describe people who are fearful of homosexuality. As a category, it helps to summarize and describe, but it is only partially descriptive of one kind of response. It leaves little room for sensitivity, acceptance, or communication. When people are labeled "homophobic," they in turn feel the negative impact of categories and, as a result, feel defensive. Obviously, this reaction helps neither the person who is categorized nor the person who categorizes.

Individuals are reluctant to deal with homosexual persons because they fear opening a Pandora's box of bewildering questions concerning human psychological development. Homosexual persons do not fulfill expected social roles and have not developed according to expected patterns of psychosexual development. Their failure to meet expectations causes us anxiety. Paul Rosenfels explains why: "The insistence of society that the inner life of the individual give way to its version of what it is to be a real man or a real woman provides an imposing bulwark against the exposure of the ignorance and immorality of the world of so-called normal people."[2]

We who can consider ourselves "normal" persons need not confront our anxieties. We who question our "normalcy" also may prefer not to confront our anxieties. But as persons and as Christians we have a responsibility to surface our anxieties, to name them as fear, to deal with them, and to grow from them. As a person who identifies himself as a helper, I have an equally important responsibility to help my clients in the therapeutic growth process toward awareness and integration of their psychological development.

Although there are reasons for anxiety concerning homosexuality and there are social and personal reasons for trying to avoid dealing with the fact that persons belong together, whatever their psychosexual development, categories and the oversimplistic way they deal with homosexuality perpetuate an attitude similar to that which maintains that blacks belong in the back of the bus and women belong in the kitchen. Blacks, women, and homosexuals belong where they are found—in society, in neighborhoods, in Church, and in religious community. The reasons for the existence and perpetuation of these attitudes, although understandable, are no longer acceptable because they reflect rigid, dated thinking.

## UTILITY OF DEFINITIONS OF HOMOSEXUALITY

The word "homosexuality," when used in psychology, generally defines a permanent psychological condition

---

2. Paul Rosenfels, *Homosexuality: The Psychology of the Creative Process* (Roslyn Heights, NY: Libra, 1971), p. 135.

whereby a man or woman is erotically attracted to persons of his or her same sex. This definition is at various times useful, necessary, and limiting.

This definition of homosexuality is useful because it helps describe the feelings and sexual attractions of individuals who either identify themselves or have experienced themselves as primarily homosexual in orientation and who struggle to live with this knowledge. This definition is particularly useful in identifying individuals who have categorized themselves prematurely and who need assistance in developing their heterosexual feelings. Such persons need to be reassured that no necessary connection exists between isolated instances of homosexual genital behavior and the so-called permanent psychological condition of homosexuality. This distinction is essential when dealing with men and women who are experiencing adolescent stages of growth during which they may have experimented with homosexual behavior.

The definition is necessary because it reflects our present state of conscious awareness. As the conscious awareness changes, so will our need for such categorical distinctions. For, as Jean Baker Miller explains: "Psychological problems are not so much caused by the unconscious, as by deprivation of full consciousness. . . . Lacking full consciousness, we create out of what is available."[3] The term "homosexuality" is the only term presently available to us to describe or to understand a certain pattern of sexual behavior. We must remember, however, that it describes the total existential picture of a homosexual individual's

3. Jean Baker Miller, *Toward a New Psychology of Women* (Boston: Beacon Press, 1976), p. 94.

personality as inadequately as any person's sexual behavior describes his or her personality.

The definition is limiting because it approaches persons as static rather than as dynamic entities. It views growth as something that can be permanently achieved rather than as an ongoing process. To the extent that any label or category influences a sense of belonging, then that label or category may militate against personal stability or security. A Jungian analyst, June Singer, maintains:

> Most people are convinced that they "belong" in one of these three categories, that they are by nature, heterosexuals, homosexuals, or bisexuals and they must accept being what they are. Or, if they cannot accept themselves as a member of a fixed category, then they conceive it their task to attempt to change themselves so they can fit. Toward this end they are willing to try any means, from aversive conditioning to cutting all attachments with the parent supposedly responsible for their being something which they do not want to be. It is my belief that these several categories, when used as labels, fix an idea in mind that need not be fixed but can be extremely fluid. We are only encapsulated in a category when we allow it to happen to us.[4]

## CONTINUUM OF SEXUAL DEVELOPMENT

In the past, psychology has considered people to be of one type or another, either homosexual or heterosexual. Today psychology suggests that people are quite capable of erotic feelings for both sexes. The word "bisexual" is used to describe these erotic feelings and activities. Singer con-

---

4. June Singer, *Androgyny: Toward a New Theory of Sexuality* (New York: Anchor Press/Doubleday, 1976), p. 278.

tends that "there are not many people who do not experience erotic feelings toward actual or potential partners of both sexes."[5] This experience is more common than we think.

Are we to conclude, then, that everyone is bisexual? Of course not, for the term "bisexual" in its classic sense refers to actual genital activity rather than to a generalized erotic attraction. Bisexual refers to people who select both male and female sexual partners. It relates primarily to genital activity with both sexes.

The bisexual category thus has much in common with the heterosexual and homosexual categories. Each focuses on interpersonal genital relationships, and because of this genital emphasis, each is inadequate when used casually by people to describe their sexual identity. All sexual categories tend to focus on genital activity or attraction, a much too narrow focus when considering the network of interpersonal relationships of which individuals may be capable.

An alternate way of perceiving sexual affect is on a continuum. We all have sexual, erotic attractions ranging from the capacity for attraction primarily to persons of the opposite sex to attraction primarily to persons of the same sex. From such a dynamic, fluid perspective, being homosexual or heterosexual is analogous to being tall or fat. Everyone falls somewhere along the continuum; everyone is a little tall or a little fat. Different societies view these places on the continuum differently. A person "belongs" in the society if his or her place is a positive one.

---

5. Ibid., p. 31.

It is neither unusual nor peculiar for a person in adolescent stages of development to experience romantic or erotic feelings toward another person of the same sex. Such feelings may also surface in religious communities, although they may not necessarily be acted on. In fact, one might argue that some homosexual affection is necessary to living in a same-sexed community. It would seem to be quite impossible for a man to live with other men or a woman to live with other women in community without some strong, positive, although not necessarily erotic, feelings of affection. Because of these strong feelings, some religious could rightly label themselves as homosexuals. But because feelings toward persons of the same sex in religious life have been discouraged by the fear of homosexuality, religious often fail to recognize the validity of deeply loving relationships with members of their own communities. This anxiety about "particular friendship" has stemmed from a fear of erotic attraction. Consequently, many religious men and women develop *no* close relationships. Certainly, the absence of feelings of belonging have much to do with the generalized deprivation of close intimate relationships in religious life.

## INTEGRATION OF THE INTRAPERSONAL

The terms "heterosexual," "bisexual," and "homosexual" refer to that aspect of sexual identity that is *interpersonal*, that is, how a man perceives himself as "masculine" and how he relates to members of his own sex and members of the opposite sex, or how a woman perceives herself as "feminine" and relates to members of her own sex and members of the opposite sex.

These terms also have stereotypic limits and fears attached to them. The *intrapersonal* is a frequently neglected dimension of sexual identity. This dimension determines how a masculine man relates to the "feminine" component of his personality or how a feminine woman relates to the "masculine" component of her total personality.

This intrapersonal aspect is described in Jungian psychology as androgyny, a category perhaps, but a more fluid one in which the process of personal integration is implicit. Androgyny "in its broadest sense can be defined as the One which contains the Two, namely the male *(andro)* and the female *(gyn)*."[6] It is, by definition, an aspect of the unconscious. Androgyny refers to a specific way of joining the "masculine" and "feminine" aspects of a single human being. Singer believes that this state of integration or wholeness has the potential "to energize the creative potency of men and women in ways that most people hardly imagine today."[7]

Moreover, Singer is convinced that "the recent expansion of androgynous consciousness, brought about largely through the catalytic effect of the Women's Movement, has increased our awareness. . . . The Women's Movement may turn out to be the decisive step in the direction of androgyny inasmuch as it confronts directly some of the obstacles that lie in the path toward androgyny."[8] If the Women's Movement is a decisive step in the direction of androgyny, then homosexuality may be yet another step

6. Ibid., p. 20.
7. Ibid., p. 22.
8. Ibid., p. 23.

forward in challenging individuals to reevaluate their conceptions of what it means to be "masculine" or "feminine." Both of these strongly felt issues can be clear challenges to personal integration at an essential level.

Every individual should be challenged to deepen and refine his or her sense of self, especially as a sexed person. A surer sense of self is a necessary step forward to deeper relationships and deeper Christian love whereby the various myths of *un*belonging can be confronted and resolved.[9]

## HOMOSEXUALITY AND BELONGING

In summary, then, homosexuality does indeed belong to each one of us in some way, and we need to change our attitudes toward it. We need to realize that it does not exist by itself, but rather is an aspect of total personality—an aspect that each one of us shares to some degree. We need to be informed. We need to reflect on how we define ourselves and on how we have been taught to define ourselves. We need to go deeper within ourselves to see the gift our anxiety has to offer us. This gift is a chance to experience our fears, our stereotypes, and our desires to grow.

During the 1960s, black people demanded their human right to sit wherever they wished on the bus. In this decade, women are demanding their human rights, a move that may prove to be in the direction of androgyny. As we move into the 1980s, homosexuals are demanding their right to be treated with human dignity and respect. Blacks do not "belong" in the back of the bus. Women do not "belong"

---

9. See, for example, Charles E. Curran, "Moral Theology, Psychiatry, and Homosexuality," *Bulletin of the National Guild of Catholic Psychiatrists* 24 (1978): 13-34.

in the kitchen. Feelings of anxiety about homosexuality do not "belong" in the closet. Myths of *un*belonging do not "belong" in Christian life. Sexuality, both hetero- and homo-, belongs to each one of us. Sexuality belongs to persons, and persons belong to themselves, to each other, and to the God who created them.

## CONCLUSION

I would like to conclude this chapter with the story of the two philosophers who were engaged in a deep discussion about where the sun goes when it sets. In the course of the discussion, they had great discourse about the possibilities, the pros, the cons, the various theories presented in the scientific literature, and recent developments in psychological understandings. As they pondered the enigma all through the night, it suddenly dawned on them.

Sister Anna Polcino, S.C.M.M., M.D., is founder and international psychiatric director of the House of Affirmation, International Therapeutic Center for Clergy and Religious, Whitinsville, Massachusetts, and instructor in psychiatry at the University of Massachusetts Medical School, Worcester. A member of the Medical Mission Sisters since 1949, Dr. Polcino received her medical degree from the Medical College of Pennsylvania. Following a surgical residency at Hahnemann Hospital, Philadelphia, she worked for nine years as a missionary surgeon and medical director at Holy Family Hospital, Karachi, West Pakistan, and Dacca, Bangladesh. She then returned to the United States and completed a psychiatric residency at Worcester State Hospital. She has received postgraduate medical education at Harvard University. A member of the American Psychiatric Association, the American Medical Association, the Massachusetts Medical Society, and the National Federation of Catholic Physicians, Dr. Polcino is current president of the National Guild of Catholic Psychiatrists.

# BELONGING—LONGING TO BE

Anna Polcino

The word "belonging" evokes one of two feelings in us, depending on our background. Some of us feel sad, even melancholy, because we have experienced so little love or affirmation in our lives or because we are struggling to discern where to belong or to whom to belong. For us, belonging is rather a longing whereby we feel lonely, deserted, rejected. Perhaps what was once present to us is now absent. Perhaps we have been near and now find ourselves far from God. Others of us, when we hear the word "belonging" feel joy, for we have been blessed with much. We belong to persons, to groups, to the Church. We have friends and a solid conviction that we are part of the lives of others.

I perceive belonging as a longing to be, longing to be a friend, longing to have a friend. Today many religious and clergy feel the need for a friend in a way that they have never felt before. The reasons for this need are many. All of us are affected by the world in which we live. Since Vatican II, many of the structures of religious life have disappeared, taking with them a certain security. In the past few years, the so-called sexual revolution has changed society's opinion of what is morally acceptable. We have been asked to get in touch with our feelings and to express our emotions openly. As a result, the apostolic demands on religious and clergy have increased, requiring heightened emotional involvement and consequent emotional pain. The workers among us are fewer; as many of our companions have left religious or priestly life, we have lost friends. Because the pace of our lives is faster, our personal involvement is more complex. The religious community we entered has undergone changes; so we are living in a way we could never have foreseen. In addition, the excitement that we experienced in the early days of dedication to our ministry, which perhaps compensated for our lack of deep relationships, is no longer with us. The daily drain of our demanding apostolic situations brings to the surface deeply felt emotional needs that we may never have experienced before. Eventually, the time comes when the tasks in themselves are not fulfilling, and we look to personal friendships for fulfillment. This need for friendship is part of every person's life. We all hunger to be more than we are, to go out of ourselves to others. Such a hunger can be fulfilled only by love, by the opportunity to touch the life of another, to love and then free that person, leaving that person better as a result of having known him or her. Many persons who long to have a friend experience problems because they do not know how to be a friend.

Christ gave us an example of friendship: ''As the Father has loved me, so I have loved you. . . . I shall not call you servants any more. . . . I call you friends. You are my friends if you do what I command you" (John 15:9-15). We know that Christ loved John in a special way, that he wept over the death of his friend Lazarus, and that he loved Mary dearly.

## SELF-ACCEPTANCE AND FEAR

Friendship implies intimacy. Religious and clergy must realize that they must accept themselves in order to have a meaningful relationship with another, even God. This acceptance depends upon our concept of self. We must reaffirm ourselves as human beings who are sexually alive. This reaffirmation is a life-long process. Some religious and clergy are afraid of friendship. Although they have developed physically and intellectually, they are stunted emotionally because they have repressed their emotions. The ability to experience a deeply personal relationship with another develops only through emotional growth. Such growth is based on self-love, the basic form of love, which makes all other loves, including friendship, possible. Only by loving ourselves can we grow to love others and the Lord.

Friendship is important for religious and clergy today. It is always good to have a friend. We have to abandon the unhealthy ways we were taught to act in the past and learn to cultivate friends. We must love others without owning, possessing, or exploiting them. We must let others come close and know us as we are while we strive to know them as they are. In so doing, we can achieve an emotional bonding or union with other persons. We know and like each other as we are, not needing genital involvement.

Certain fears can act as psychological blocks to friendship. These fears include: (1) fear of sexuality, including
fear of sexual "contamination," and sexual inadequacy;
(2) fear of anger and increased irritability (As two people
reveal themselves more intimately to each other, they will
find that they are not perfect. Thus we must deal with
anger in close relationships.); (3) fear of dependent relationships (Many of us cannot permit ourselves to need, to
show weakness. Thus much promiscuity is a struggle of
one person to dominate another.); (4) fear of intense feelings of personal inadequacy, which can make us hide our
true selves and wear masks or play roles in interpersonal
contact; and (5) the fear of being vulnerable or hurt, when
the intimacy of real friendship demands that we permit
ourselves to be weak and vulnerable. Some of these psychological blocks may require professional help, but solitary reflection that gives us insight into and an understanding of ourselves helps, and is often enough.

## INTENTIONAL FRIENDSHIP, NOT COUPLING

Coupling is the model in society today. Our first experience of it occurs as we view the coupling of our parents. In
coupling, there is a giving over and a taking, an entry into
another and a leaving of self. In coupling, each person
both experiences a new freedom through a common unity
and abandons a certain freedom through a sexual oneness.
Two spirits, two bodies, two emotions become one. Each
surrenders to the other and compromises to preserve the
oneness. The two must exclude others because there are
dimensions that cannot be shared.

Coupling cannot be the model for religious and clergy.
For us, the model must be intentional friendship, whereby

the two establish an open bonding, relinquishing possession. They together share no one dimension that they cannot share with another. The friendship is always open to others; it is not exclusive, but rather inclusive. Complementarity is the dynamic of this unity. Because the two celibates have sacrificed the freedom to establish their oneness in flesh, they are free to enjoy each other as the separate persons they are. Their fidelity to one another rests entirely on trust. There is no ownership. The two may crave physical bonding, but they do not need it.

Religious and clergy who are the model for this type of friendship do not ask how far they can go, for they recognize their commitment. Friendship cannot be legislated. A strong embrace will lead to other acts only between some persons. The quality of the individual commitment determines the course of the friendship. Intentional friends appreciate the uniqueness of each other; they do not need to make the changes that would result in oneness. As they remain the two together, they cannot soothe each other physically as couples do, but they can trust each other and remain faithful to that trust.

## THE SPIRIT OF CELIBATE FRIENDSHIP

Models for celibate friendship between men and women can be found in Church history: Clare and Francis of Assisi, Teresa of Avila and John of the Cross, Jane Frances de Chantal and Francis de Sales. These saints were able to realize great things for the glory of God at least partially because of their friendship. In the earlier days of the Church, such friendships were praised and considered very much in keeping with the Christian spirit. Today we must recapture that spirit of celibate friendship.

A friendship is not something we shop for. A gift from God, it comes quietly and slowly. Like all gifts from the Lord, it is not for the two friends alone; it should nourish the total lives and apostolates of both. Through the friendship, God is asking for more dedication and more commitment to him and to his people. The two friends treat each other with respect, and they support each other. They help each other to become more honest, more open, more transparent before God. The goals of their lives, not their desire to remain geographically close to one another, are the determining factors in their choice of apostolate and in their openness to mission.

Although we can long for friendship, we cannot create a friendship. But we can create an atmosphere conducive to receiving this gift when it comes. In Church history, one can also find unhealthy friendships. We must be aware of such pitfalls and be honest with ourselves, for we cannot live double lives.

Johan Rake has described friendship as "an encounter between two or more persons in a mutual sharing of space and time, embodied in a given culture, involving interaction and communion in light of some interest in one another and in shared truth or shared search for truth, resulting in an enduring nonexclusive relation which is lived as a gift of affinity, affection and personal history, and occasioning the autonomous growth of the person involved."[1]

---

1. Johan Michele Rake, "Friendship: A Fundamental Description," *Humanitas* 6 (Fall 1970): 175.

## ACCEPTING OUR SEXUAL
## AND EMOTIONAL NATURES

We Americans are considered friendly people, but while we may be good at casual relationships, we are not necessarily good at forming deep friendships. Sometimes we cannot form such relationships because we do not recognize and accept our emotions. We may instead deny them or reject them. But to avoid pain is to miss an opportunity to grow. We religious and clergy often grow intellectually but not emotionally. Our education and formation provided us with knowledge we could impart. We acquired skills so we could share the truths we were learning about God, human beings, and the world in which we live. But today, instead of being asked to serve people by supplying them with truth or answers to the problems they face, we are being asked to communicate with them personally and individually. We are being asked to listen to their needs, to share their struggles, to allow them to know our deepest attitudes, values, faith experiences, struggles, and weaknesses.

This challenge brings with it problems that arise from the sexual and emotional natures that God has designed for us. Our sexuality is an integral part of our lives. Every one of our interior and exterior activities has a sexual aspect. It is impossible for human beings to be asexual in anything they do, including communicating with God. All of us in the Church owe it to God, as our Creator, and to ourselves to accept the maleness or femaleness he has given us. We must recognize the sexual aspect of all that goes on within us, especially within the context of our inter-personal relationships. In our culture, when people use the

term "sexuality" they really mean "genitality." Genitality
actually refers to the arousal or use of the genital parts of
the human body. We religious and clergy have made a free
choice not to use the genital aspects of our nature. But we
cannot as a result give up our sexuality.

One of the difficulties of living the celibate life is the
spontaneous and indeliberate arousal of genital feelings
and desires. We religious and clergy know that our relationships with certain persons whom we find humanly ap-
pealing tend to produce at times more or less strong genital
reactions within us. Moments of such feelings are inescap-
able in the context of the apostolic, shared, deeply transparent lives we experience in intimate contact with men
and women and God. While we must struggle to achieve
impulse control, we may experience such feelings as ten-
derness or as the warmth of a heart filled with gratitude,
friendship, or love. These feelings are partly psychological
and partly physical. They are also closely related to our
thoughts and our imaginations, which elicit affective responses. These responses include our feelings, emotions,
passions, and moods. (Feelings are mild emotions; passions are very intense ones. Moods are the emotional states
in which we remain for a certain period of time.) Affective
response is as essential an aspect of our humanness as is
our sexuality. We have to be affective to be human.

We might ask what we should do with our genital sexual
reactions, for being celibate must have a positive value and
not be simply a condition of our work. Some celibates use
their celibacy as an excuse for avoiding intimacy. Some of
these celibates even have genital relations and still avoid
intimacy. They exhibit a typical pattern of genital contact,
repentance, breaking up with the other, renewing commit-

ment to vocation, and then genital involvement with yet another. Whether acknowledged or not, such involvement is intentional. The celibate is acting out an emotional or sexual problem.

Being chaste is a difficult virtue for all of us. We must be realistic about our sexuality. We must not fear it, but we should acknowledge our individual fragility. Close friends must intend to remain celibate (chaste). They need to know that they want male-female intentional friendship, not a marital or quasi-marital relationship—not coupling. Something besides the relationship must be at the center of the friends' hearts. If one or the other friend or both experience a desire for sexual expression, the friends know that every desire need not be acted upon. If problems arise, the two must be open about the relationship. Being secretive creates a seductive atmosphere. Rash judgments from fellow celibates can encourage secretiveness. The relationship should be kept in the open so it can be understood by the community. Because our cultural value system is in such a state of change and because so many persons have left ministry, we tend to pull back and to grasp any safe way of living and dealing with the issues. Without real support systems, we turn a need for healthy privacy and growth into secrecy. We tend to support those who behave similar to the way we behave and to criticize those who do not. It is difficult to support someone who is risking and struggling in a relationship of which we do not approve. Yet lack of support is one reason why we fail to communicate and to be open about our relationships.

All of us must cultivate a giving self and a receiving self. I love you because you are you and I am I, and it is good for us to be ourselves together. We need to develop the androgynous center of our being, our animus-masculine and anima-feminine qualities.

## DIFFERENT TYPES OF FRIENDSHIP

We must understand the confusion about the meaning of friendship today if we are to develop real friendships, intentional friendships. We need to know the dangers that can weaken, pervert, or transform our friendships into some other kind of relationship. For instance, Dale Carnegie's advice that we can make more friends in two months by becoming interested in other people than we can in two years by trying to get other people interested in us suggests that we can make true friends instantly. Carnegie also recommends telling people only what they want to hear. This advice confuses friends and admirers or fans. Making friends requires time and truth.

Often we do not distinguish among fans, collaborators, friendly acquaintances, pals, and true friends. Sometimes we assume that a friend is someone who knows us and still likes us. This assumption reduces a complex relationship to what is an occasional feeling and distorts our awareness of the full reality. At other times we identify a friend as one who satisfies our needs. But another person is greater than his or her usefulness to us. We take more than the person has to offer: we meet the person for what he or she is.

Aristotle distinguished three types of relationships that we generally regard as friendships. The first is friendship based on utility, which is sustained as long as the relationship proves to be useful. The second is friendship founded on pleasure, which disintegrates when one party is no longer entertained or amused by the other. The third kind of friendship exists between good men who are alike in excellence or virtue. Aristotle maintained that the first two types of friendship can be enjoyed, but should not be accepted as substitutes for true friendship. We should recognize that many of the people we name as friends are simply people we enjoy, or enjoy using, or who provide occasional companionship to help us avoid loneliness. I agree with Aristotle that there is a third kind of relationship called friendship, and I believe that it is essentially a form of love.

## THE LOVE OF FRIENDSHIP

Love is neither a special kind of feeling (eros, affection, or gratification of a felt need) nor a particular kind of concern or action, but a special kind of relationship between two persons. Two individuals within the bond of love discover and realize both their oneness and their freedom. Two persons become one, but are sustained as two persons. They affirm each other. To regard love from the viewpoint of one individual is to distort it. There is much emphasis, particularly in theological literature, on the unitive power of love. Too often the creative power of love is overlooked. We celibates can be co-creators. Love is an interpersonal relationship that can develop the best in persons and enable them to formulate appropriate identities, discover new dimensions of freedom, develop mature and responsible consciences, and give shape to hopeful, human worlds. Love is not just a special kind of feeling found in erotic or romantic natures or a merging of two personalities into one. It is an indispensable factor in personal growth toward full maturity.

When we love, we experience mutual trust; we feel free to relax and be ourselves. We feel at home with another person; we feel that we belong. Those who experience romantic and marital love are liberated from isolation so that they discover the freedom to be one. We who chose intentional friendship form a bond that allows us the freedom to be two. The danger is that one of us may assert dominance over the other or that we both may idolize our union so that it blinds us to the rest of reality, so that we share infatuation instead of love.

The Greeks invented a special word for friendship love, *philia*. Aristotle said of true *philia* that no man would choose to live without friends if he had all other goods. Friendship is an end in itself: to be a good friend, one must be morally good. To become a good friend, one must be another's equal and prove himself or herself worthy of friendship. Aristotle also saw love as an extension of self-love: "A man is his own best friend. . . . Therefore he should have the greatest affection for himself." Aristotle identified the highest form of friendship as the love of wisdom, whereby one is alone, contemplating truth known through the mind, but ignoring the truth known in the heart. I disagree, for Christ taught us that we must listen to the truth known in the heart.

Speaking to his apostles as friends, Christ emphasized their freedom. He told them that they shall know the truth, and that the truth will set them free. Through loving one another, we experience mutual indwelling. We also are willing to sacrifice, suffer, and even die for our friends.

Thomas Aquinas affirmed that when we love another person, the good we seek is not our own but the good of our friend, for the friend's sake. When we love, we strive for insight into the friend's soul, so that our relationship can be characterized by knowledge as well as goodwill and affection.

Dante also celebrated the love of friendship. Virgil is Dante's friend who affirms his dignity and freedom. The most horrible punishment inflicted upon any of the damned in *The Inferno* is for betraying the bond of friendship.

During the Reformation, Luther and Calvin undermined the faith in human nature that is essential for the development of friendship by stressing the corruption of man's nature. What mattered to them was what goes on between the believer and God. They made no room for the concept of love as a relationship between friends. The subsequent Protestant work ethic left us no time to develop and enjoy close friendships.[2] In modern society, working relationships have become more important than personal relationships, and I-thou relationships have been overwhelmed with I-it attitudes. The value placed on success has led to an emphasis on individual achievement; keeping busy; lucrative productivity; effective manipulation of data, programs, and personnel; exotic experiences; and security of moral certainty that in our striving we are doing what is right. In addition, our geographical mobility deters friends from spending time together enjoying each other.

## CHARACTERISTICS OF HEALTHY FRIENDSHIP

We must appreciate what it means to have and to be a true friend if we are to develop a humane and hopeful

---

2. I am greatly indebted to William A. Sadler, Jr., "The Experience of Friendship," *Humanitas* 6 (Fall 1970): 177-209, for the above discussion of Aristotle and others.

world. William A. Sadler, Jr. identifies five characteristics of healthy friendship:[3]

1. *Joy*. When good friends meet, especially if they have been separated for some time, they share a special kind of happiness that we rightly identify as joy. Friends are delighted to see each other and to relax in the enjoyment of each other's presence. They will laugh easily and frequently and are willing to share their joy with others, to enlarge the circle of friends. Friends also feel contentment when they share in a meaningful experience. If they are unable to share such an experience, they realize that the experience would have been even more meaningful if they had been able to share it.

2. *Communion*. Friends know that their relationship is held together by more than an equal satisfying of each other's needs. They know that their bond is sharing life's more meaningful moments, its suffering and struggles, its triumph and elation. Friends develop a sense of communion when they pursue a common interest, when they cooperate and share responsibilities in a project, or when they simply play. They need not have identical interests. After a long separation, friends who were once very close may find that their friendship has changed. This change occurs because the friends have not sustained a common life. They can renew or rebuild the friendship by establishing communion. One way to establish communion is to engage in intimate conversation. Close friends can express their convictions, their worries, and their deepest questions to one another; they can also relate their most secret experiences because they trust one another. Whereas sexual inter-

---

3. Ibid., pp. 197-208.

course is the consummation of romantic love, heart-to-heart conversation is the consummation of friendship. Both actions are personally fulfilling only if both persons seek to know what the other is.

Communion requires attentiveness, openness, and gentle sensitivity. We all experience loneliness, the feeling of being in a world where we are homeless. Loneliness is different from solitude, which is time lived quietly, contentedly alone, thinking, reading, looking, or listening. We should learn to enjoy solitude and to resist the temptations of loneliness. Rather than sense that people are essentially isolated from each other, we can sense a developing consciousness of our singular identity, in its distance from the environment and humanity in general. Friends can assure us of this identity, but we must not ask them to protect us from loneliness. If we do so, our friends become objects that satisfy our need for companionship. Friendship bestows communion that enables us to face loneliness with courage and the awareness that we are not totally alone in our world.

3. *Freedom.* The work of love is creative: it strengthens and liberates the individuals who love. If love is genuinely creative, then when we are loved we are changed, and we should expect those we love to have new strengths, new interests, and a keen appetite to pursue those interests. Love must be open to the other and be for the development of the other. It also must be ready for constant readjustment to the growth of the other.

Discovery is another gift of love. We will experience moments of surprise and discovery as newly emergent aspects of the other's personality become manifest. Such discovery is often a testimony to the liberating effect of love.

Encouraged by friendship, persons will tend to exercise their freedom in the direction of personal development, expanding their horizons and actualizing latent potentialities.

Anxiety makes us uncertain and afraid, but a good friend provides us with feelings of worth and trust. When we are anxious or discouraged, we are apt to lose faith in others, in the environment, and in ourselves. We cannot open up and give ourselves to new possibilities. But when friends express faith in us, we are freed from some of the crippling effects of anxiety, for our friends accept us as we are. With our friends we do not have to compete to prove ourselves better than we really are. Yet if a friend's faith is genuine, it is not blind. If our friends pretend that our misdeeds do not exist, or if they ignore the facts of some of our foolish, selfish actions, then they do not really know us. If they acknowledge a wrong action and yet have faith in us, they will not condemn us but will know us as we are.

Forgiveness is an essential part of friendship, and Jesus was one of the first to express this truth. To be a friend means that we meet our friends not only with faith that affirms their freedom, but with forgiveness that releases them from a guilt that would inhibit their human action. Our freedom extends only as far as the horizon of our personal world. As we participate in the worlds of others, the size of our personal world increases. Thus an increase of freedom through faith, forgiveness, and mutual sharing in an interpersonal world that enlarges our own horizons is an essential element in friendship.

4. *Truth.* In friendship we speak of truth. Our friends may tell us that what we intend to do is inconsistent with our best purposes and character. They may tell us that what we have done is wrong. Their voices are our second

conscience, based on an understanding of us and our situation that is both objective and sympathetic. We are fortunate if we have friends to help us reach important decisions. A friend's judgment, honestly rendered and sympathetically expressed, can free us from self-deception, for the judgment is truth spoken in love. Friends not only encourage each other to be true to themselves and to each other, but also to live consistently with their truth when meeting social responsibilities. In particular, friendship encourages us to transform this world into the kind of place in which the values of friendship, such as love, freedom, and truth, will be honored.

As friends speak to us in truth, they help us to become aware of the persons that we are and might become. They help us sense our identities as whole persons. When we speak the truth to our friends, we discover a true vision of life and its possibilities.

5. *Sacrifice.* To share in another's life, we must be willing to sacrifice and suffer. Whenever we become involved with another person whose identity and freedom it is important for us to affirm, we must be prepared to sacrifice self-assertion and selfishness. To respond to a friend's call, we must say no, at least momentarily, to interests, plans, and activities that are important to us. This surrender is not a loss but an expression of freedom for the sake of our friends and our friendships. To have communion with friends, we must sacrifice some of our aggressive tendencies and peculiar desires or genital stirrings. When we love, both joy and suffering may be conditions of our relationship.

These characteristics constitute a skeleton of friendship, the proportions of which will differ as friends and friendships differ. The relationships that priests and religious develop are often service-oriented and functional without ever becoming deeply personal. Yet it is only through deep personal relationships that we come to know ourselves as we really are and learn to deal with our feelings honestly and maturely. After all, the call to celibacy is a call to become fully human by going ever deeper into life.

## FALLING IN LOVE

In the psychosexual development of life, everyone must go through the adolescent stage and experience infatuation. Many priests and religious who entered early, even during late adolescence (up to age 27), may not have experienced falling in love. Because they were no longer in contact with the opposite sex once they entered priestly or religious life, their growth was stunted. Thus priests and religious may find themselves falling in love at age 40 or 50. They will recognize it for what it is, and they may feel guilty, not because they have acted out physically, but because of their fantasies. The two involved in this friendship have to talk honestly and distance themselves. If an embrace evokes genital feelings, then it should be avoided.

No amount of personal commitment to an ideal of celibate chastity will automatically prevent a person from falling in love. When priests and religious recognize their real feelings of attraction and affection for another person, they may naturally feel guilty for having compromised their vows. These feelings flow from their background and training. We must therefore realize that most people fall in love a number of times in life and that what is important is how the experience of falling in love is dealt with and integrated into previous life commitments. In a friendship between a married lay person and a priest or religious, each person has a previous commitment—the lay person to the married partner, the priest or religious to God. Each person should respect the choice of the other. Our celibacy and our communities are part of who we are. The other loves this wholeness. We priests and religious would not be ourselves without it. In a healthy friendship, the married person who sees his or her priest or religious friend becoming estranged from commitment to God and community will remind his or her friend about the prior commitment. Fellow priests or religious should also invite the friend to look at his or her commitment. True friends love one another's wholeness. They help one another struggle with who each is, remembering who each has been in the past and who each had hoped to be in the future. If friends use this suffering as an opportunity to offer one another oneness elsewhere, with each other, they are no longer friends.

We cannot condemn people for their feelings. The fascination of coupling can become intense, particularly among priests and religious who never experienced the normal adolescent infatuation that is part of our emotional development. But true intentional friendship means more than one friend. The celibate should have many friends, for multiple friendship is one way in which coupling and intentional friendship differ. There will be times when friends are no longer present. But the memory of friendships and the growth they brought will always remain. These memories and our relationship with Christ will sustain us.

The following comments can serve as guidelines for male-female relationships in general and for celibate-lay person and celibate-celibate relationships in particular.

1. Both persons need a high degree of self-knowledge. Immature persons are often very clumsy in developing such relationships. Self-knowledge is most important.

2. The persons must be selective about the individuals with whom they form a special friendship. Do not seek friendships with unhappy persons. Friendships should be between persons happy with their lives, their life styles, and their deliberate life choices.

3. Relationships must be consistent with a person's celibate commitment and life style.

4. Caution signs include: erotic manifestations, resentment when others are present, demanding responses such as "drop everything and everyone and be present to me," community or rectory life suffering because of a one-to-one relationship, and relationships that lead to an erosion of interior prayer and spiritual realities.

Friendship enables us to become simultaneously aware of our riches and our poverty. We are not long in realizing that what we possess is far inferior to what we would like to give our friends. We must therefore continue to grow, and in large part it will be the generosity of our friends that will enable us to increase our riches, both on the level of having and on the level of being. True friendship is possible only when we recognize and accept the differences that distinguish us from others. By making ourselves more available to others, we become more and more ourselves. In friendship we discover and reveal what we are and, perhaps still more, what we are capable of becoming. It is normal for friends to influence one another. But when we influence our friends, we need not communicate our own riches; rather we should make our friends discover their own riches. This is the greatest gift we can give to others. It follows then that friendship demands discretion, disinterest and forgetfulness of self, and renunciation of self-love.

Whatever the dangers, it is my firm conviction that friendship between celibate men and women is not an impossible ideal. But it can be realized only between persons who have attained a relatively high degree of spirituality and whose higher values are very much in evidence.

Moreover, friendship does not necessarily last forever. We will lose friends through death and prolonged physical separation. Other persons may come between us, or our friends may betray us. Everything human is fragile, the degree of fragility depending upon the individuals and their situations. Persons sharing even the most beautiful friendships often have an obscure feeling that they are not understood and loved absolutely. Yet, despite its imperfections and limitations, friendship is one of the most precious values of the human condition.

## BELONGING TO OUR FRIENDS AND TO GOD

Still, because of its limitations, friendship will never fully satisfy the human heart. As Augustine said, "You have made our hearts for you, O God, and they are restless until they rest in you." All that I have said about the value of human friendship should be applied to our friendship with God. Joy, communion, truth, freedom, and sacrifice are inherent in our friendship with God. There will be times in our lives when we have only God. For that reason, we must develop a deep life of prayer that must be worked at, just as every human relationship must be worked at. The mystery of the human person with whom we are friends can become our basis for approaching the mystery of God.

The reality of God can be described as a mysterious shared goal of friends. So celibate friendship can contribute to a vision of God as the ultimate mystery of love, sometimes present and sometimes absent, always moving toward a very personal love, to be sought as the common goal and hope of life. The process of becoming will lead to belonging. We cannot be detached if we have not known attachment. In turn, integrating this nonpossessiveness brings not only personal benefits to those involved, but enrichment to the whole Church and the world by its witness to mystery, love, and hope in God. Thus we celibates can be this model for friendship. Thus our sense of longing to be becomes a belonging both to our friends and to God.

Sister Virginia O'Reilly, O.P., Ph.D., is a full-time psychotherapist at the House of Affirmation in Montara, California. A member of the Adrian Dominican Sisters since 1944, Sister O'Reilly received her doctorate in clinical and developmental psychology from the California School of Professional Psychology, San Francisco. She was awarded a Danforth Foundation Graduate Fellowship for Women to support these studies. Sister O'Reilly did her undergraduate studies at Barry College, Miami, Florida, and holds graduate degrees from the Catholic University of America and from Siena Heights College, Adrian, Michigan. She has done additional graduate studies at various colleges and universities throughout the United States. Prior to joining the staff of the House of Affirmation, she was an educator, a guidance counselor, and the founding Director of Studies for the Adrian Dominican Congregation. She has worked as a consultant to the Center for Applied Research in the Apostolate (CARA) and has been active on the Sisters Council Executive Board of the Archdiocese of San Francisco. She is a Fellow of the Society for Values in Higher Education and a member of the California State Psychological Association, the National Assembly of Women Religious (NAWR), and Network, a religious lobby in Washington, D.C.

# BELONGING TO SELF: ROOTEDNESS THROUGH THE PROCESS OF MID-LIFE INDIVIDUATION

Virginia O'Reilly

My thoughts these days are of trees, those majestic reachers-to-the-skies whose most awesome representatives are found in the mists of the redwood groves of the Pacific coast. Trees seem to me to symbolize the maturity of the person's middle years. Like a person, a tree reveals the source of life by its very being and presence. In Thomas Merton's poetic phrasing, a tree "spreads out toward what it loves, and is heliotropic. . . . A tree grows out into a free form, an organic form. It is never ideal, only free: never typical, always individual."[1] In order for a tree to achieve its full stature, its roots in the hidden depths underground must expand and deepen to support the height and breadth of the mature tree above ground.

---

1.Thomas Merton, *The Secular Journal of Thomas Merton* (New York: 1959), p. 24, as quoted in Herbert C. Burke, "The Man of Letters," *Continuum* 7 (Summer 1969): 276.

In my therapeutic work with professional religious persons, I have found that such persons tend to escape confrontation with the inner world of the self by taking neurotic flight to the service of the other—or, at least, by giving lip-service to the service of the other. When I point out this tendency to the persons who exhibit it, they perceive my insights as an attack on the value system we share rather than as a mutual focusing of attention on a neurotic pattern that in fact destroys a healthy religious life style. After one such person cried out to me, "You are trying to get me to be selfish!," I decided to link the psychological development of the adult with the Christian development of the professional religious, in an effort to give a credible cognitive framework to the process of growth toward human, Christian maturity.

Rev. Barry McLaughlin points out that psychological maturity and growth in grace are not mutually dependent:

> The natural possibility facilitates the supernatural process, but there can be psychological maturity where there is theological immaturity. On the other hand, a person can live in the presence of God and perform virtuous actions while at the same time manifesting a certain psychological infantilism indicative of a defect in human development rather than a lack of response to God's grace.[2]

Yet the maxim "grace builds on nature" teaches that the full flowering of the mature Christian life depends, to some extent, on full human development, at least within the usual ordering of providence. St. Paul tells us: "We are God's work of art, created in Christ Jesus to live the good

2. Barry McLaughlin, *Nature, Grace and Religious Development* (New York: Paulist Press Deus Books, 1964), p. 103.

life as from the beginning he had meant us to live it"
(Eph. 1:10). Rev. Thomas F. O'Meara comments on the
way a Christian is meant to give witness to the faith within:

> Preaching for the individual Christian consists in the
> quality of his life, and this life is the word of life. It is
> neither composed of distinctly Christian actions, nor
> of compulsive "good works." Rather, the Christian's
> life is to stand out as something striking, beautiful,
> attractive.[3]

O'Meara uses the argument of Rev. Jerome Murphy-
O'Connor, professor at the Ecole Biblique in Jerusalem, to
clarify the Pauline notion of witness:

> Paul was convinced that Christian witness is given
> within the context of normal social activity . . . we are
> rather inclined to forget that the basic idea of the In-
> carnation is that *we must become men.* Acceptance of
> this fundamental point is basic to the idea of witness,
> for only the activity of fully mature and complete
> human beings can have the quality on which Paul lays
> emphasis.[4]

I would not want to conclude that so-called maturity is a
prerequisite to effective Christian witness, for each of us
lives within certain givens, certain limitations of culture,
family, and education. We cannot change what we are, nor
the past that nurtured us. But as we consider what we can
become, what we are in the process of becoming as we
grow and develop toward Christian maturity, we must
assume the burden of addressing both the natural and the

---

3. Thomas F. O'Meara, *Holiness and Radicalism in Religious Life* (New York: Herder and Herder, 1970), p. 134.
4. Jerome Murphy-O'Connor, "Religious Life as Witness," *Supplement to Doctrine and Life,* 17 (1967): 124ff., as quoted in O'Meara.

supernatural aids available. McLaughlin explains:

The goal of religious transformation is the possession of that mind which was in Christ Jesus (Phil. 2:5). Yet as the religious man comes in contact with the channels of God's grace, gaining confidence and strength in his spiritual commitment, he frequently finds that there are psychological obstacles and deeply rooted attitudes preventing the rational and free expression of personal decision which normally provides the basis for the higher achievements of supernatural life. Spiritual directors are coming to realize that faith is strongest in an integrated, well-adjusted, emotionally healthy individual. The person who comes to understand the previously unknown and unconscious sources of his motivation is more free and responsible and, consequently, capable of higher sanctity.[5]

## THE MIDDLE YEARS: A TIME FOR INDIVIDUATION

Only recently have psychologists addressed themselves to the developmental processes that occur during adulthood.[6] Roger L. Gould, M.D., a major contemporary theorist in this discipline, notes that:

. . . mid-life is the time for resolution: we abandon old conspiracies, overcome remaining internal prohibitions and correct whatever distortions, misperceptions and misunderstandings that have prevented us from becoming authentic, whole people.[7]

---

5. McLaughlin, p. 120.

6. Cf. Virginia O'Reilly, "Relationships in the Middle Years," in *Intimacy: Issues of Emotional Living in an Age of Stress for Clergy and Religious,* ed. Anna Polcino, M.D. (Whitinsville, MA: Affirmation Books, 1978), pp. 74-78.

7. Roger L. Gould, *Transformations: Growth and Change in Adult Life* (New York: Simon and Schuster, 1978), p. 293.

Persons who are devoted to the goal of transforming themselves into personalities that reflect the mind of Christ Jesus (Phil. 2:5) and who have in fact oriented themselves with all their hearts and minds in that direction since adolescence or early adulthood may be dismayed to find that much work remains to be done. Those persons who have spent little time meditating on the Gospel instructions (Matt. 22:39) for loving others may benefit from the words of William Johnston:

> . . . most of us live in illusion about ourselves and other people because we project upon ourselves and others the archetypes from our own unconscious. And to escape from ignorance and illusion we must discover the real self hidden below the stream of hate, fear, aggression, anger, lust, arrogance and so on passing across the mind.[8]

Professional religious are unlikely to experience consciously this "stream of hate, fear . . . and so on" and may in fact deny the presence of these emotions in themselves, so effective has been their effort of will across the years to deny such negative affect expression in conscious motivation and choices. Yet we all share certain basic characteristics of human nature. Carl Jung theorizes that among these characteristics are the contents of the collective unconscious, the *shadow:*

> The shadow is a moral problem that challenges the whole ego personality, for no one can become conscious of the shadow without considerable moral effort. To become conscious of it involves recognizing the dark aspects of the personality as present and real. This act is the essential condition for any kind of self-

8. William Johnston, *The Still Point: Reflections on Zen and Christian Mysticism* (New York: Harper and Row, 1971), p. 60.

knowledge, and it therefore, as a rule, meets with considerable resistance.[9]

Rev. Henri de Lubac has said: "Everytime man gives up a particular way of thinking, he fears he is losing God."[10] Loyal professional religious complain that there is too much attention on psychology and not enough emphasis on traditional theology. As it happens, this concept of the *shadow* has respectable links with traditional theology. Rev. Victor White explains:

> Man's fallen and disintegrated condition, the disorder of desires *(concupiscentia inordinata)* and the lust of spirit against flesh, and of flesh against spirit, must be humbly accepted if they are to be transmuted. . . . There is no escape from the world, flesh and devil: they are to be renounced only by being faced and overcome. Jung only echoes the teaching of Christian writers . . . when he insists that the first step on the way to reintegration—which the Christian understands as conformity to the pattern of Christ—is the recognition and acceptance of the "shadow". . . . grace does not rid us of the shadow, but prevents our being dominated by it.[11]

Others also cite this need for attention to personal integration, for the development of the unique individuality that is my personal reflection of the limitless characteristics of the divine. Rev. John LaFarge has said that "perhaps the highest homage to truth is the ability to recognize one's

9. Violet S. de Laszlo, ed., *Psyche and Symbol: A Selection from the Writings of C. G. Jung* (Garden City, NY: Doubleday Anchor Books, 1958), pp. 6-7.

10. Henri de Lubac, as quoted in O'Meara, p. 122.

11. Victor White, *God and the Unconscious* (Chicago: Henry Regnery, 1953), pp. 79-80.

own personal limitations."[12] But recognition of limitations is only part of growth toward individuality; freedom within the accepted limitations is also necessary. Carl Rogers says that the mark of maturity is openness to experience and that, as this openness increases, the less predictable a person's behavior will be.[13] Although the person's behavior will be dependably appropriate, it will not be rigidly patterned.

Adrian van Kaam tells us that the essence of spirituality is graced originality.[14] He develops this theme of attentiveness to our origins, to our originality, as a way of achieving an experiential awareness of the working out of God's will for each of us:

> God's Will appears everywhere. It is first of all in me, in everything I am and do. I must "catch" the Divine Will at work in myself. I must find it at the root of my thoughts, feelings, actions. Each time I arrive at the originating source of action, emotion, reflection, I am faced with a unique manifestation of God's preserving and allowing will. I can rest in this Ground. I can quietly participate in the sustaining and originating Divine Will at the base of what I think, feel and do.[15]

12. John LaFarge, as quoted in McLaughlin, p. 100.
13. Carl R. Rogers, "The Concept of the Fully Functioning Person," *Psychotherapy: Theory, Research and Practice* 1 (August 1963): 17-26, as quoted in Philip D. Cristantiello, "Psychosexual Maturity in Celibate Development," *Review for Religious* 37 (September 1978): 650.
14. Adrian van Kaam, *On Being Yourself: Reflections on Spirituality and Originality* (Denville, NJ: Dimension Books, 1972), p. 114.
15. Ibid., pp. 133-34.

Daniel J. Levinson describes the psychological task of individuation as the characteristic developmental task of the middle years:

As Jung conceived the term, as it is commonly used by psychologists, individuation is a developmental process through which a person becomes more uniquely individual. Acquiring a clearer and fuller identity of his own, he becomes better able to utilize his inner resources and pursue his own aims. He generates new levels of awareness, meaning and understanding. Individuation is known to be a crucial aspect of development in childhood and adolescence. Jung was the first to recognize that individuation occurs, and is sorely needed, at mid-life and beyond.

Until the late thirties, says Jung, a man's life is of necessity rather one-sided and imbalanced. Many valuable aspects of the self have been neglected or suppressed. Of the four psychological functions—thought, feeling, intuition and sensation—that all personalities must exercise, only one or two are likely to have developed much. Although no one develops all four functions to an equal degree, it is possible in middle adulthood to strengthen the formerly weaker functions and to lead a more balanced life.

Mid-life individuation enables us to reduce the tyranny of both the demands that society places on us and the demands of our own repressed (instinctual) unconscious. We can begin giving more attention to what Jung calls the "archetypal unconscious" an inner source of self-definition and satisfaction. Archetypes are, so to speak, a treasury of seeds within the self. Most of them remain dormant in early adulthood. Through the process of individuation in middle adulthood, as a man nourishes the archetypal figures, and gives them a more valued place in his life, they will evolve and enrich his life in ways hardly dreamed of in youth. Individuation is not without painful transitions and recurrent setbacks, but it holds the possibility of continuing self-renewal and creative involvement in one's own and others' lives.[16]

We come now to the "how": what aspects of life are accessible to our own efforts to belong more fully to ourselves, to search out those roots of our thoughts, actions, and feelings that are the "Ground" of our being, the deep places of our origin that sustain the being and presence that show what has been the source of life? Levinson suggests that a re-integration of four basic polarities present in the human personality throughout development will assist the individual toward a more uniquely expressive sense of self. He lists these polarities as: young/old, destruction/creation, masculine/feminine, and attachment/separateness. He states:

> Each of these pairs forms a polarity in the sense that the two terms represent opposing tendencies or conditions. Superficially, it would appear that a person has to be one or the other and cannot be both. In actuality, however, the paired tendencies are not mutually exclusive. Both sides of each polarity coexist within every self. At mid-life, a man feels young in many respects, but he also has a sense of being old. . . . His developmental task is to make sense of this condition of in-between and to become Young/Old in a new way, different from early adulthood. The Destructive/Creation polarity presents similar problems of conflict and reintegration. . . . In middle adulthood a man can come to know, more than ever before, that powerful forces of destructiveness and of creativity coexist in the human soul—in my soul—and can integrate them in

16. Daniel J. Levinson, *The Seasons of a Man's Life* (New York: Alfred A. Knopf, 1978), pp. 328-30.

new ways. Likewise, every man at mid-life must come
more fully to terms with the coexistence of masculine
and feminine parts of the self. And he must integrate
his powerful need for attachment to others with his
antithetical but equally important need for
separateness.[17]

Levinson emphasizes that these polarities are part of a
man's life; that is, they are not simply internal matters, existing within the self, but are also in the society in which
that self dwells. He says: "As individuation progresses, a
person not only becomes internally more differentiated
and complex: he also develops more effective boundaries
that link him to the external world and enable him to trans-
act with it more fully."[18]

The polarities that Levinson identifies are the result of
his study of the lives of contemporary American men. In
the remainder of this chapter, I intend to link these
polarities to aspects of the spiritual life. Whether this exercise proves meaningful will be determined by each reader's
personal search of his or her own life experience. I have
found the linkage an exciting theoretical framework, and I
invite the reader to explore it with me.

## INDIVIDUATION ALONG THE
## POLARITY OF YOUNG/OLD

As women and men of the Church, we need in the middle years to be able to let go of earlier, less adult forms of
consciousness in order to be open to what Rev. Roger
Haight describes as a "theology and vision of the Church
that corresponds to our historical consciousness, concern

---

17. Ibid., p. 197.
18. Ibid., p. 198.

for the concrete conditions and needs of people in this world, and the pragmatic hope that our Church will make a difference in their lives."[19] The personal task of individuation that makes it possible for women and men of the Church to face with mature and sober dedication the work of "making a difference" is to let go of "the distortions of childhood consciousness and its demons and protective devices that restrict our life."[20] Gould maintains:

> As our life experience builds, ideally we abandon unwarranted expectations, rigid rules and inflexible roles. We come to be owners of our own selves, with a fuller, more independent adult consciousness. We live by a world view generated out of personal experience, not one dictated by our need for protection. As we feel more "adult," we correct our own excessive infant demands, and abandon the need for complete control and ownership of the loving mother. . . . We are no longer dependent, powerless children, and we can now view life from the independent vista of adulthood.[21]

But at mid-life the process of individuation requires that we do more than relinquish the dream of youth. As a tree "spreads out toward what it loves, and is heliotropic," each ecclesial woman and man opens to new understandings, new visions, and a "firmer sense of who he is and what matters to him."[22] Each person must open thus for himself or herself, in a fashion "never ideal, only free:

---

19. Roger Haight, "Mission Spirituality," an address given at the General Chapter of the Adrian Dominican Sisters, Adrian, Michigan, December 27, 1977, p. 6.
20. Gould, p. 37.
21. Ibid., pp. 37-38.
22. Levinson, p. 217.

never typical, only individual.''[23] The creation of the middle-aged self, ''wiser and more mature than before yet still connected to the youthful sources of energy, imagination and daring,''[24] has been lovingly described by Pierre Teilhard de Chardin:

> It was a joy to me, Lord, in the midst of my struggles, to feel that in growing to my own fulfillment I was increasing your hold on me: it was a joy to me, beneath the inward burgeoning of life and amidst the unfolding of events that favored me, to surrender myself to your providence. And now that I have discovered the joy of turning every increase into a way of making—or allowing—your presence to grow in me, I beg of you, bring me to a serene acceptance of that final phase of communion with you in which I shall attain to possession of you by diminishing within you.[25]

## INDIVIDUATION ALONG THE POLARITY OF DESTRUCTION/CREATION

The murky depths of the unconscious and semiconscious part of the human personality contain those characteristics of the individual that are experienced as ''not-I.'' Although not welcomed within the bright circle of conscious motivation and choice, the unacknowledged and unwelcome internal destructive forces are often the hidden shoals on which the best efforts of the conscious personality flounder. Unless these destructive forces are acknowledged, understood, and allowed for, they tend to assume a life and influence of their own, outside of the conscious

---

23. Merton, p. 24.
24. Ibid.
25. Pierre Teilhard de Chardin, *Hymn of the Universe* (New York: Harper and Row, 1961), p. 103.

control of the individual, but capable of creating chaos nonetheless.

If the presence of the destructive tendencies in human nature (that is, our heritage from the original parents, Adam and Eve) can be faced with sober maturity, the process of limiting and containing the effects of these tendencies may be addressed and the integration of these dark aspects into the total personality begun. All major writers of the spiritual life appear to have understood that an integration is an essential and necessary precondition to full development of a form of Christian life known as mystical prayer. In his discussion of the process, William Johnston, commenting on John of the Cross, tells us:

> . . . the silent mystical prayer has been thrusting down into the depths of the soul, extending the horizon of consciousness and integrating unconscious elements. . . . it is not impossible that these trials of John of the Cross . . . take place, in many cases, at a definite period of life; that is to say, in Jung's "middle period of life," a time of psychic toil and trouble. . . . This is the age of the spiritualization of the personality, of what Jung calls a "transformation of nature" into culture, or instinct into spirit; and, if all goes well, it points to a coming interiority, hitherto unknown. . . . and at this time Jung . . . urges that one be calm; quietly allowing nature to take its course and effect the spiritualization of the personality.[26]

One of the great struggles of the personality is the acceptance of death, both the death of the body and the death of those aspects of the self that are the precondition for an increased capacity to be creative, loving, and affirming of

---

26. Johnston, pp. 36-37.

life. The familiar notion that the seed must die in order for
new life to issue from it is used by Rev. George A. Maloney
to describe this tension:

> Each Christian in Baptism becomes a seed implanted
> into the Church. There he is to grow to full maturity.
> . . . A *transfiguring* process is taking place over the
> spring, summer and autumn years of the Christian's
> life. . . . endowed with the power of the Trinitarian life
> imbedded into his being in Baptism, [the Christian] is
> being driven by God's inner activity and man's
> cooperation towards the fullness destined for him in
> Christ Jesus. The Christian's growth is a movement in
> assimilating love that divinizes as it both unites and
> distinguishes man in his uniqueness because of his con-
> sciousness that God loves him uniquely. . . . The "two
> hands of God," Jesus Christ and His Holy Spirit, to
> use St. Irenaeus' apt analogy, are continuously
> touching the soul, releasing new energies that are one
> with God's uncreated energies. These energies were
> there before, but now a *transforming* process has taken
> place.[27]

In earlier developmental periods, the perception that
destructiveness is a force outside the individual, against
which a heroic struggle must be waged, predominates.
During the middle years, however, we attempt to
assimilate a tragic sense of life, which "derives from the
realization that great misfortunes and failures are not
merely imposed upon us from without, but are largely the
result of our own tragic flaws."[28] Much of the great
literature of the world, from *Oedipus Rex*, to *King Lear*
and the contemporary *Death of a Salesman*, focuses on a

27. George A. Maloney, *The Breath of the Mystic* (Denville,
NJ: Dimension Books, 1974), pp. 175-76, 178.
28. Levinson, p. 225.

theme in which the hero does not "attain his original aspirations" but "is, however, ultimately victorious: he confronts his profound inner faults, accepts them as part of himself and of humanity, and is to some degree transformed into a nobler person. The personal transformation outweighs the worldly defeat and suffering."[29] Teilhard de Chardin describes how, for the Christian, it is the very agent of defeat that is the source of a new creation:

> In the Christian vision, the great triumph of the Creator and Redeemer is to have transformed into an essential agent of life-bestowal what in itself is a universal power of diminishment and extinction. If God is definitively to enter us, he must in some way hollow us out, empty us, so as to make room for himself. And if we are to be assimilated into him, he must first break down the molecules of our being so as to recast and remold us. It is the function of death to make the necessary opening into our inmost selves.[30]

## INDIVIDUATION ALONG THE POLARITY OF MASCULINE/FEMININE

Since we live in a youth-oriented culture, we are surrounded by stereotypic representatives of what it means to be masculine or feminine. In early adulthood, the reproductive tasks of men and women encourage the expression of either the masculine or feminine component of the individual personality. Later, the need to inhibit the opposite polarity, felt strongly during early adulthood, is relaxed, and it becomes more acceptable to relate to the various

29. Ibid., p. 226.
30. Teilhard de Chardin, pp. 129-30.

archetypal figures of maleness and femaleness in a new way that makes the masculine and feminine components less rigidly separated in the personality. Levinson says: "The developmental task is to come to terms in new ways with the basic meanings of masculinity and femininity."[31]

I must confess that I find it difficult to delineate the implications that such an individualization may have for ecclesial women and men. We are at present so far from even being conscious of the deprivation that women and men experience because of the patriarchal symbols in which our religious heritage has been transmitted that it is extremely difficult to envision the consequences of a relationship with the Divine that is freed of the cultural sexual stereotypes in which it was originally formulated and promulgated. Yet this religious heritage has freed itself from the concepts that slavery and war are legitimate, and these concepts were part of that same cultural formulation. Mary Daly describes her hope for a fuller possession of the common humanity of both sexes should such a freedom develop:

> Women and men inhabit different worlds. Even though these are profoundly related emotionally, physically, economically, socially, there is a wall that is visible to those who *almost have managed* to achieve genuine interplanetary communication with the opposite sex. The prerequisite of this achievement is communication within the divided self, discovery of the lost self. The adequate meeting of the two worlds, then, cannot be imagined as a simple one-to-one relationship between representatives of humanity's two halves, for half a person really never can meet the

---

31. Levinson, p. 236.

objectified other half. The adequate "cosmosis" will require a breakdown of walls within the male psyche as well as within the female. It will require in men as well as in women a desire to become androgynous, that is, to become themselves. Whenever men manage to see this promise in themselves of actually finding themselves, of finally agreeing with themselves, they will have reached the threshold of the new space. . . . If they do not shrink from the good news because it means a loss of undeserved privilege and prestige or because it means setting forth on a long and perilous trip into uncharted territory, they might succeed in becoming human.[32]

Rev. Bernard J. Bush has attempted to describe the influence of patriarchal symbols on religious formulations,[33] but much more work along this line remains to be done, especially on the influence of archetypal images on the formulation of theological dicta by male theologians.

## INDIVIDUATION ALONG THE POLARITY OF ATTACHMENT/SEPARATENESS

Levinson states that "a major developmental task of middle adulthood is to find a better balance between the needs of the self and the needs of society."[34] He explains this balance thus:

A man who attends more to the self, who becomes less tyrannized by his ambitions, dependencies and passions, can be involved with other individuals and perform his social roles in a more responsible way than

32. Mary Daly, *Beyond God the Father* (Boston: Beacon Press, 1973), pp. 171-72.
33. Bernard J. Bush, "I Have Called You By Name," in Polcino, pp. 43-45.
34. Levinson, p. 242.

ever before. He can respond more to the developmental needs of his offspring and other young adults if he is more in touch with his own self and responding to its needs. He can develop greater wisdom if he is less focused upon the acquisition of specific skills, knowledge and rewards. In order to care more deeply for others, he must come to care more deeply for himself. Caring means that he is mainly concerned not with material comfort and success, but with self-development and integrity. It means that he will exercise authority with greater imagination and compassion. It means that while he enjoys the power and tangible rewards of leadership, he gains even greater satisfaction from creating a legacy, enjoying the intrinsic pleasures of work and having more individualized, loving relationships. . . . He can be more loving, sensual, authentic, intimate, solitary—more attached and more separate.[35]

This "attention to the self" has a long tradition in Christianity: ". . . the mystical descent is made into the deepest realms of the soul where God is—or more daringly and correctly, which is God. For John of the Cross says that the center of the soul *is* God."[36] That such a descent allows the Christian to renew the process of "attachment," to adapt, to participate in or master the external world while at the same time preparing to leave it, detach from it, was clear to Teilhard de Chardin:

It is a truly christian duty to grow, even in the eyes of men, and make one's talents bear fruit, even though they be natural. It is part of the essentially Catholic vi-

---

35. Ibid., pp. 242-43.
36. Johnston, p. 75. Cf. St. John of the Cross, *Living Flame of Love*, trans. and ed. E. Allison Peers (Garden City, NY: Image Books, 1962), pp. 39-40.

sion to look upon the world as maturing—not only in each individual or in each nation, but in the whole human race—a specific power of knowing and loving whose transfigured term is charity, but whose roots and elemental sap lie in the discovery and love of everything that is true and beautiful in creation. . . . the effort of mankind, even in realms inaccurately called profane, must, in the christian life, assume the role of a holy and unifying operation. . . . Understood in this way, the care which we devote to personal achievement and embellishment is no more than a gift begun. And that is why the attachment to creatures which it appears to denote melts imperceptibly into complete detachment. . . . Up to a certain point the believer, who, understanding the christian meaning of development, has worked to mould himself and the world for God, will hardly need to hear the second injunction before beginning to obey it. Anyone whose aim, in conquering the earth, has really begun to subject a little more matter to spirit has, surely, begun to take leave of himself at the same time as taking possession of himself.[37]

## SUMMARY

I began this investigation in an attempt to link the psychological development of the mature adult to the Christian development of the professional religious person. A tree analogy was used to help conceptualize the need for a deep rootedness in the personality if the balance and symmetry and source of life are to be preserved. Some concepts from the psychological theories of Carl Jung were used for illustration although such theories are admittedly

---

37. Pierre Teilhard de Chardin, *Le Milieu Divin* (London: Fontana Books, 1964), p. 97.

useful only in attempting to understand what is occurring naturally in the person. White reminds us:

> It is precisely that relevance of faith and practice to the needs and workings of the human psyche that Jung's psychology appears to have rediscovered. . . . It does not claim to sow, still less to explain or explain away, the Gospel seed: but it does inform us about its effects in the soil that receives it, and upon the soil's condition which enables the seed to live or die.[38]

We need not be surprised that the process of growth in the earlier periods of development leaves imbalances to be adjusted in the middle years. Teilhard de Chardin has said:

> It would be surprising to find, in a bouquet, flowers which were ill-formed or sickly, since these are picked one by one, and artificially grouped together in a bunch. But on a tree which has had to struggle against inner accidents of its own development and external accidents of climate, the broken branches, the torn leaves, and the dried or sickly or wilted blossoms have their place: they reveal to us the greater or lesser difficulty encountered by the tree itself in its growth.[39]

Our effort at investigation of the rootedness that helps us belong to ourselves, to develop that uniqueness which is the goal of the mid-life effort at individualization, has led deep into the personality.

> Yet growth in the spiritual life consists simply in extending the supernatural into the realm of the natural so that it permeates life. The only access to God is personal and active commitment. In this way the thoughts of God become gradually assimilated, until there is no evaluation, no decision, no thought which does not have its roots in God. For it is only from the light

---

38. White, p. 69.
39. Teilhard de Chardin, p. 114.

which streams constantly from heaven, as Simone Weil once wrote, that a tree derives the energy to strike its roots deep into the soil. In fact, the tree is rooted in the sky.[40]

---

40. McLaughlin, p. 113.

*All income derived from the sale of this book goes to no individual but is applied to providing care for priests and religious suffering from emotional unrest.*

AFFIRMATION BOOKS is an important part of the ministry of the House of Affirmation, International Therapeutic Center for Clergy and Religious, founded by Sr. Anna Polcino, S.C.M.M., M.D.